Career Training and Personal Planning
for Students with Autism Spectrum Disorders

of related interest

Career Success of Disabled High-Flyers
Sonali Shah
ISBN 1 84310 208 0

Realizing the College Dream with Autism or Asperger Syndrome
A Parent's Guide to Student Success
Ann Palmer
ISBN 1 84310 801 1

How to Find Work that Works for People with Asperger Syndrome
The Ultimate Guide for Getting People with Asperger Syndrome into the Workplace
(and keeping them there!)
Gail Hawkins
ISBN 1 84310 151 3

Employment for Individuals with Asperger Syndrome or Non-Verbal Learning Disability
Stories and Strategies
Yvona Fast and others
ISBN 1 84310 766 X

Succeeding in College with Asperger Syndrome
A Student Guide
John Harpur, Maria Lawlor and Michael Fitzgerald
ISBN 1 84310 201 3

Managing with Asperger Syndrome
Malcolm Johnson
ISBN 1 84310 199 8

Career Training and Personal Planning for Students with Autism Spectrum Disorders

A Practical Resource for Schools

Vicki Lundine and Catherine Smith

Foreword by Jo-Anne Seip

Jessica Kingsley Publishers
London and Philadelphia

First published in 2006
by Jessica Kingsley Publishers
116 Pentonville Road
London N1 9JB, UK
and
400 Market Street, Suite 400
Philadelphia, PA 19106, USA

www.jkp.com

Library of Congress Cataloging in Publication Data

Lundine, Vicki, 1949-
   Career training and personal planning for students with autism spectrum disorders : a practical resource for schools / Vicki Lundine and Catherine Smith ; foreword by Jo-Anne Seip.
      p. cm.
   ISBN-13: 978-1-84310-440-7 (pbk.)
   ISBN-10: 1-84310-440-7 (pbk.)
   1. Autistic youth--Education. 2. Autistic youth--Employment. 3. Career education. 4. School-to-work transition.
I. Smith, Catherine, 1948- II. Title.
   LC4717.5.L86 2006
   371.94--dc22
                                                                2006008071

British Library Cataloguing in Publication Data

A CIP catalogue record for this book is available from the British Library

ISBN-13: 978 1 84310 440 7
ISBN-10: 1 84310 440 7

Printed and bound in Great Britain by
Printwise (Haverhill) Ltd, Suffolk

Contents

Acknowledgments

We wish to thank the students who participated in, and are currently participating in, the program. We would like to acknowledge the partnership established with parents, which is not only an essential element to a successful program, but has proven invaluable. Employers have provided meaningful work experiences for our students as well as constructive criticism for improving student participation in the workplace. We would also like to recognize the teachers, para-professionals (e.g. teaching assistants, educational assistants), and individuals in community agencies who have supported students throughout this process. Ian Grant, a teacher in the program from its inception, continues to foster talents in every student with whom he comes in contact. Ray Hughes, now retired, was the District Assistant Superintendent of Special Education when the program began. Not only did he support the initiative to start the program, he was instrumental in establishing the position that insured that all students, including those with special needs, gain access to career education and work placement opportunities in the community. Jo-Anne Seip, founder of the Provincial Outreach Program for Autism and Related Disorders in British Columbia, has supported students, parents and teachers in understanding the challenges and talents of these young adults through her consultations, training and mentoring. Clara Clairborne Park, her husband David and their daughter Jessy continue to provide insights, guidance and encouragement to the authors. In her books *The Siege: The first eight years of an autistic child* (1967) and *Exiting Nirvana: A daughter's life with autism* (2001), Clara aptly demonstrates that by beginning with an end in mind, and fostering individual talents and interests, much can be accomplished. Bill Standeven, Ministry of Education, British Columbia, has been a constant support in our vision that all students are entitled to experience opportunities to access the workplace. We would like to thank the British Columbian Ministry for Education for permission to use their terms for organizing information and evidence for a career portfolio, as well as their career portfolio headings (see themes on page 155). These are from the *Graduation Portfolio Workbook* (www.autismoutreach.ca). Pat Czuczor's belief that the program should be shared with parents and professionals motivated the authors to pursue this project. Pat Czuczor, Jason Scharf and Maggie Scherf encouraged, proof-read and formatted the manuscript. We would like to thank Rita John, BSN RN, who is the Health Promotion Advisor for Powell River School District, for her valuable insights and experiences in developing the Personal Peak Safety Program. Jason Scharf has been most generous in designing the Personal Peak Graphics for the manual. Without the extensive collaboration on the part of many dedicated individuals, this project would never have come to fruition.

Foreword

Over the past 15 years, research in the field of autism spectrum disorders (ASDs) has led to an explosion of written materials focusing on the etiology of these disorders and the many therapies and interventions recommended to parents and educators. Much of the focus for educators has been placed on assessment, behavior management, communication, social skills training, curriculum planning and implementation of educational programs that parallel the traditional curriculum for normal same-aged peers. Seldom is an educator able to find a text or manual designed specifically to address the skills necessary to insure success in the adult world of work. All too frequently, young people with ASD are leaving secondary school without the skills necessary to enable them to find and retain employment, live independent lives and be afforded the same opportunities as their neurotypical peers.

As an educator involved in the provision of services to secondary-school-aged children with ASD for the past 30 years, my saddest moments have been the telephone calls from parents asking if their child who recently "graduated" from a secondary school could now register in our school program in order to learn functional skills that would make him or her employable and/or able to live independently in their home community.

I take great pleasure in having the opportunity to write a foreword for this book, as the contents run contrary to the sad outcomes described above. Central to this book is the notion that classroom teachers, parents and school teams can work together toward developing the talents of children with autism spectrum disorders to insure success in the world of work and adulthood.

This book provides guidelines for placing students in "real work" experiences and clearly defines the role of the parent, the school team, the job coach and the employer. Teachers and other readers will find the contents straightforward and direct. Lesson plans, practical applications and well defined implementation procedures provide the classroom teacher and parents with the tools necessary to insure success.

Throughout each chapter, instructional and teaching procedures, materials needed to teach the specific skill(s), data collection procedures, checklists and evaluative measures are clearly defined. Chapter Seven is particularly applicable to school districts that are in the process of developing career portfolio units for all students preparing to leave the school system. The authors provide teachers with a series of lessons that can be used to enable students with ASD to fulfill the requirements for the graduation portfolio which is now a prerequisite for graduation in the province of British Columbia.

This book is a "must" read for teachers of students with ASD. I would also recommend it as required reading for parents and other professionals involved with secondary-aged students with an autism spectrum disorder.

Jo-Anne Seip, M. Ed.
Administrator
Provincial Outreach Program for Autism and Related Disorders
BC, Canada

Introduction

This book evolved as a result of a course that was developed in 1993 in Campbell River, British Columbia, Canada. The course was designed to teach students with autism and other developmental disabilities employment and personal planning skills. This manual offers teachers and parents a scope of issues that need to be addressed by parents, teachers, community support workers, and employers in order to enhance employment opportunities for these young adults. It covers a series of skills which all students leaving school, including those with learning challenges, should know and be comfortable applying, and provides activities that teachers can use with the group, as well as worksheets for students to complete with the class, in a small group, with a peer, or independently. Providing students with opportunities to participate in work placements during the course often leads to relevant issues that arise which can be discussed in the group, thereby benefiting everyone. These real-life experiences allow the teacher to revisit and reinforce concepts and strategies addressed in the curriculum.

The course covers topics designed to help students increase their understanding of themselves and the world around them. The lessons concentrate on helping students acquire strategies that will enhance participation in their communities and develop skills that lead to healthy lifestyles and meaningful employment. It is recommended that the topics be taught over two or three years to insure that students are not only introduced to concepts, but, through review and maintenance schedules, begin to internalize the concepts so that they can truly apply what they have learned.

Before starting the course, teachers should become familiar with the material as a whole. Although the chapters are organized in a progressive format, they can be taught in the order that best meets the needs of the students as a group. The authors would like to bring Chapter Seven, "Career Portfolios: A Demonstration of Skills, Attitudes and Abilities," to the teacher's attention. Teachers may wish to introduce elements of this chapter early in the course and revisit the chapter regularly, particularly if the course is taught over an extended period.

The appendix contains a checklist of all the topics covered to help maintain accurate records for the student. It also contains samples of agreements and questionnaires that students can practice completing.

Chapter One

Overview

This book has been designed as an instructional tool to provide teachers and parents with a work experience curriculum for individuals with autism spectrum disorders (ASDs) and other developmental disabilities. Topics and skills are clearly defined so that each member of a child's team can work toward supporting and developing the talents necessary to insure success in the workplace. A healthy work ethic begins at a very early age. Parent and teacher expectations can positively influence a healthy and well rounded individual who is preparing to enter the world of work. Initially, the team should clearly define each member's roles and responsibilities to help foster the student's skills, attitudes and knowledge about work. Team members can agree to:

- recognize when a student successfully completes a task, whether that task involves washing the dishes at home or handing in completed assignments at school

- reward with positive reinforcements. Praise on its own or accompanied by such rewards as stickers or a token economy system can help promote an intrinsic understanding of the meaning of responsibility

- insure that the student has adequate opportunities to carry out responsibilities in the home and at school. This helps to promote cooperation and accountability

- provide positive feedback and constructive criticism. These are important ways of promoting independence and critical awareness of what it means to do a good job.

In addition to teaching specific skills, students will be taught to recognize potential job opportunities available to them in the community. As partners in teaching, parents will be asked to encourage their children to observe people at work, visit different work sites, and talk to friends, relatives and neighbors about the types of work that they do. As the single most important influence in a child's life, parents will be encouraged to advocate for their son or daughter and help provide opportunities to practice work skills at home, in the neighborhood, and in community settings such as church, clubs, and volunteer organizations. Acknowledging and understanding the strengths, interests and talents of individual students and encouraging them to experience a variety of job opportunities will help build confidence and expose them to more environments to demonstrate the skills they are learning. Being visible also enhances community awareness of the potential of these students and the benefits in hiring them.

The goals of career development for all students, including those with ASD and developmental disabilities, are:

- self-exploration and assessment

- development of skills related to more independent living and employability

- career awareness

- career exploration

- career preparation.

Guidelines for placing students with ASD and other developmental disabilities in community work placement

In recognition of the need to facilitate positive work experiences for students with ASD and other developmental disabilities, the following guidelines have been developed for school districts and employers in the community:

Each student should have:

1. an Individual Education Program (IEP) that outlines:

    - the goals of the work experience

    - the purpose of the work experience

    - the anticipated outcomes of the work experience

    - how the work experience will be measured in terms of success for the student and the community

    - how the work experience relates to future career plans for the student

2. an assessment of interests and skills that includes a description of his or her physical, social and academic abilities

3. a guarantee that the Special Services Department and/or school will provide the necessary support systems the student requires while on work experience placement

4. an agreement from the parent/guardian of the student to participate in the process of establishing and supporting an appropriate work experience.

Following the completion of the above, and in consultation with the student, parent, teacher, counselor and the administration, the career facilitator will make arrangements for an appropriate work experience for the student.

Procedures for placement of students with ASD and developmental disabilities
STUDENTS IN RESOURCE ROOM PLACEMENTS

1. The classroom teacher discusses the program with the student.

2. The School Career Facilitator works with the classroom teacher to insure that all the paperwork is complete before the District Career Facilitator is called.

3. The District Career Facilitator meets with the IEP team to discuss the work experience in more detail.

4. If the student requires a para-professional to accompany him or her to the work site, the arrangements for the para-professional must be made by the classroom teacher prior to the work experience being arranged.

5. The District Career Facilitator makes arrangements for an appropriate work placement and reports back to the classroom teacher and the student.

6. The District Career Facilitator takes the student and para-professional, if one is assigned, to the placement interview.

7. The District Career Facilitator does the site visitations unless there are special circumstances which warrant the School Career Facilitator making the visits.

8. The District Career Facilitator is responsible for thanking the employer.

STUDENTS WITH SEVERE LEARNING DISABILITY (LD)/HIGH-FUNCTIONING AUTISM (HFA)/ ASPERGER SYNDROME (AS)

1. School and/or career counselors discuss the program with the student.

2. The student is introduced to and interviewed by the School Career Facilitator. At this point the student is informed that he or she will be meeting with the District Career Facilitator to discuss the work experience placement in more detail.

3. If the student requires a para-professional to accompany him or her to the work site, the arrangements for the para-professional must be made by the school prior to the work experience being arranged.

4. The School Career Facilitator works with the classroom teacher to insure that all the paperwork is complete before the District Career Facilitator is contacted.

5. The District Career Facilitator meets with the teacher and the School Career Facilitator to discuss each student's supports that may be required, the objectives for the student, transportation, parent contact and any special circumstances.

6. The District Career Facilitator meets with the School Career Facilitator and the student. When the student has established a rapport with the District Career Facilitator, the School Career Facilitator should leave. This allows the District Career Facilitator to establish a relationship with the student as he or she will be accompanying the student to the job interview and to the work site.

7. The District Career Facilitator makes arrangements for an appropriate work placement and relays information back to the classroom teacher and student.

8. The District Career Facilitator takes the student and the para-professional to the placement interview.

9. The District Career Facilitator makes the site visitations unless there are special circumstances which warrant the School Career Facilitator making the visits.

10. The District Career Facilitator is responsible for the thank-you letter to the employer.

The role of parents

> The family remains the primary influence, advocate and educator in the development of their child's attitudes, standards and values.
>
> (Gregg Hill, Campbell River and District Association
> for Community Living, in an interview, 2004)

Parents play a pivotal role in helping their son or daughter develop the values and foundation skills required to experience success in their future careers. It is the parents who initiate recruiting the support their child requires to begin their journey as a dynamic and unique participant in the community. Accessing support early in the child's development is essential. Celebrating a child's strengths and recognizing his or her challenges are important steps in the process. Each goal that is achieved encourages greater independence, mobility and recognition in the community. It remains important that parents continue to understand which skills and knowledge their child requires in order to maintain and enhance their access to a fulfilling life. The support of qualified professionals, including speech and language therapists, physiotherapists, occupational therapists, teachers trained in the field of special education and teachers trained in career education, can all provide parents with information that helps determine priorities, interventions and processes their child will require to prepare him or her for participation in the community. Teams that practice effective collaboration strategies tend to create rich and realistic opportunities for the student.

In addition to collaborating with the school team, it is important that parents recognize that many students with ASD and other developmental disabilities need to be trained to observe the world that surrounds them. Experience has taught us that we should never assume, because we notice where we are and what visual signals abound in the environment to provide us with information, that the individuals with whom we work are aware of any of it. Teach your child to look around, to observe and to question if he or she appears uncertain about what he or she is seeing or experiencing. Walk around the neighborhood and attempt to see what your child sees. Does he or she:

- notice the street signs?

- listen for sounds in the environment?

- recognize when something is different?

- read the numbers on the houses or recognize a block parent sign? (Block parents are volunteers who work with the local police precinct to insure the safety of children in their neighborhoods. They have training and support from the police and post a sign on their house or in their windows to let children know they can seek assistance there.)

- look up and around?

Actively teaching skills can significantly enhance the individual's success in the workplace. Establish routines that address the need for order and cleanliness around the house, the apartment, the hallway outside the door, or in the yard. These skills can transfer to recognizing when something is out of place, missing or dangerous in the home or on a work site.

The next time you go shopping, check to see if your child recognizes fast-food logos. There are some signs your child may recognize automatically. However, he or she may have difficulty recognizing "In," "Out," "Enter," "Exit,"

"Danger," "No Admittance," "Closed," "Women," "Men." Why this discrepancy? Just consider how many millions of dollars advertising agents have spent on making sure individuals see and hear their logo and themes thousands of times a year so that the majority of people pay attention to their product. We need to teach children to recognize and understand signs and information in order to increase their safety and independence. The ability to look around, process the available information, and assess the environment is a very important life skill.

Not only do we need to teach individuals to look around for cues in the environment, we also need to help them to listen to their environment. Attempt to heighten their awareness of the sounds they hear. Along with recognizing the sounds in the environment, parents should be especially conscious of teaching their children to learn to recognize sounds that potentially affect their safety. Oncoming cars, buses, trucks, trucks backing up, horns, sirens and construction sounds are all potential hazards when a child is not conscious of the meaning attached to them. If we can train children to hear the approaching vehicle or recognize that there is construction under way, we can also teach them to prepare for the action they may need to take to remain safe and in control.

Job preparedness begins early. Establishing joint attention, commenting on joint activities, demonstrating good manners and participating in household responsibilities are all a part of learning how to be a socially responsible individual. Simple skills such as putting dishes in the dish washer, making a bed, taking the garbage out, cutting lawns, washing windows, maintaining good hygiene, greeting people, answering the phone and taking messages are but a few of the common courtesies that help prepare individuals for being appreciated in a community setting. By establishing clear expectations and routines, parents can create essential foundations for the type of citizens that employers and communities value.

Parents can appreciate that career training begins at home, partners with the school system and continues after students graduate. Career development is a lifelong pursuit. Having opportunities to access responsible curriculum, supportive staff, and work experience opportunities during the school years can significantly influence a child's independence in the years that follow.

Leadership in the school

A student's success in acquiring work skills is significantly influenced by the team's ability to collaborate. Parents know their individual child. Teachers and administrators understand the child as a member of the community of learners. Together, parents, teachers and administrators can help create a meaningful IEP that encourages growth, development and satisfaction.

When a team collaborates, it has the opportunity to prioritize the skills a student will need to learn to complement the lifestyle he or she would like to pursue. Meaningful collaboration also implies that the team will schedule the time to dialogue about the skills a student can practice across environments. This is important because active collaboration increases the student's opportunities to rehearse the skills until they become an intrinsic response. Remember how much time and energy major corporations spend to repeat the same message over and over until one begins to respond automatically. There is wisdom in the theory that educators should concentrate on teaching more, less (Smith 1969). In other words, insure that students are:

- learning those critical skills which support their growth and development

- practicing those skills across people and environments

- given enough time and opportunities to establish a foundation on which to build more sophisticated skills.

Instead of attempting to teach an inordinate number of skills over a designated time-frame, be selective and provide the time for the student to learn essential skills well. Review the student's progress regularly. Determine whether the goals and objectives remain priorities that will continue to enhance and support the student's strengths, interests and talents.

The school as a training ground

Schools provide a rich environment where students enrolled in a functional curriculum can begin to practice some of the skills that require intense training over an extended period of time for the student to succeed. These jobs can begin in the elementary grades. When children with ASD or other developmental disabilities are asked to assume responsibility for certain jobs in the school, it is because those jobs will enhance that student's ability to master and generalize the skills being practiced. Routinely performing relevant and functional tasks helps students who require hands-on experience to perfect their skills. These teaching opportunities help students acquire basic concepts that are the foundation for further learning. As valuable basic concepts are mastered, more challenging and complex skills can be added to their repertoire.

As an example, consider the task of collecting attendance. If each class in a school or section of a school were numbered, the student and an assistant could paste the corresponding number on a sleeve that could be posted next to the classroom door in the hallway. Each morning the classroom teachers would place their attendance slip in the sleeve. The student would carry a clipboard with a sheet bearing the numbers that correspond to the classroom numbers. Place a laminated sheet over the sheet with the numbers on it. On the back of the clipboard create a sleeve that the student would put the attendance slips in as he or she collects them. The student could learn to trace over the numbers to indicate that he had picked up the attendance. This repetition and practice encourages learning the numbers, how to write them, their order and one-to-one correlation. Over time, the numbers on the collection form can be dotted, and as the child learns the sequence and demonstrates mastery, the child can independently mark the corresponding class numbers. This activity could facilitate desensitizing the child when the prospect of transition to a new classroom is imminent. When a teacher does not have the attendance ready, the child can learn to knock, wait, ask for the slip, thank the teacher and quietly close the door. There are a variety of skills that can be created around this seemingly simple task. The pictures and names of the teachers can be added to the sleeve. Depending on the ability of the child, he or she can learn to recognize teachers' faces and read their names. Learning to recognize and communicate with substitute teachers can also become a part of the teaching process. Another benefit to collecting attendance includes increasing the child's comfort level with the school environment.

When the attendance has been collected, the attendance sheets can then be taken to a quiet location where the child can count the number of children absent in each class, using one stick to represent each child absent. She or he can put the sticks into a container and at the end bundle them into groups of ten. A chart indicating how many children are absent can be created and shared with the class at the end of the week or the month. Peers can be asked to hypothesize as to why some days there were a lot of children absent, such as Halloween. This activity can increase peer interactions. It can also heighten peer appreciation for the skills and talents the child with special needs is acquiring.

A functional curriculum that includes jobs that can be performed in the school setting allows students to participate in real work that fosters the development of real skills. It remains important for the team to:

- prioritize the skills the student needs to learn
- establish the process
- consider how to increase the level of difficulty
- recognize when it is time to abandon the activity
- determine how to assess success
- plan how to generalize the skills the student learned.

Refer to the appendix for some school responsibilities that have been developed by special education teacher Ian Grant of the Campbell River School District in British Columbia, Canada.

The role of the employer

Students with ASD and other developmental disabilities continue to face attitudinal barriers in employment. The mentoring process involved in a work experience can help break down employment barriers by encouraging individuals with challenges to take a more active role in planning and pursuing their careers. This program helps provide employers with access to new talent and an often under-utilized workforce. Once employers begin working with a person with a disability, they soon recognize the person's capabilities rather than the disability. The experience can have an impact on everyone at the work site. Mentoring individuals with disabilities can help an organization broaden its understanding as it learns to look beyond labels.

The employer begins by receiving a student's resumé. This is followed by an interview. During the interview process, the employer provides the student with the necessary information he or she will need to begin work:

- explanation of appropriate clothing

- starting and ending dates of the work experience

- hours of the work experience

- safety issues and equipment

- specific duties.

During the work experience the employer can then:

- provide training

- assist in the development of learning objectives for the student

- encourage positive attitudes toward work

- develop student awareness of community values

- network with the student for future employment

- evaluate the work experience.

The employer plays a major role in the education of all students. By providing opportunities, support, and encouragement, employers enable students to prepare for their careers by introducing them to real jobs in the real world.

The employers who have become partners in educating students with special needs do so because they honestly believe in "giving someone a chance who may not have otherwise had the opportunity. It is the right thing to do." (Rod Holter, VP of Operations for Eclipse Aviation)

Employers who become committed partners in training provide important feedback to the student. Employers also make important recommendations for improving the process that enables students to experience meaningful participation on the work site.

Enhancing the environment

Establishing a safe, supportive environment is crucial to help facilitate learning for students with special needs. A teacher should always be prepared. The goals and objectives that are being taught should be clearly established well ahead of time. Materials should be available. Parents and guardians should have an outline and knowledge of the topics and skills so that they can provide their son or daughter with the material supports that may enhance their participation. Parents can also help establish opportunities for practicing and generalizing skills.

Students should be made aware that the classroom is a private place where sensitive topics and personal experiences will be discussed. It will also be a place to develop problem-solving strategies. The topics of confidentiality, respect, understanding and support should be discussed in the initial classes, and revisited as very sensitive topics such as sexuality and challenges in the workplace are discussed.

Students with developmental disabilities encounter communication challenges. Students with ASD experience challenges in the areas of receptive, expressive and pragmatic communication skills. These are inherent features of the diagnosis. Communication is complex. It is multifaceted and it is an essential element that underlies the ability to socialize. All students with communication challenges can benefit from the support of a qualified speech and language pathologist to help facilitate student success and to support the community in understanding and facilitating access for these individuals.

Visual strategies are powerful tools that enable these individuals to understand and learn concepts. Visual supports and organizers:

- provide individuals with ASD with effective and powerful means of communication

- provide references that enhance organization

- encourage increased independence, security and control

- teach a child what to do

- establish boundaries

- help shape and teach desired behaviors.

Temple Grandin (2000) states that "Thinking in language and words is alien to me. I think totally in pictures... In autism, the systems that process visual-spatial problems are intact. There is a possibility that these systems may be expanded to compensate for deficits in language."

Insure that concepts which are delivered verbally are supported by graphic organizers, illustrations, videos, PowerPoint presentations, photos and demonstrations.

The role of job coaches

Definition

A job coach is a para-professional who facilitates a student's maximum independence in the workplace.

This means:

- demonstrating respect at all times for the student as a responsible young adult

- taking a back seat when going on an interview with the work experience teacher

- being unobtrusive in the workplace – cueing, monitoring safety, providing support only when required and keeping that as subtle as possible

- acting as a reinforcing pair of ears and eyes as needed

- looking professional

- showing up on the job site with the necessary tools for monitoring student progress: clipboard for marking behaviors and objectives, task analysis sheets, writing notepaper to record environmental obstacles and communication or personal safety issues that may need to be addressed

- remaining the silent partner on the job

- training the student to remain conscientious about the physical set-up

- prompting students to be aware of other jobs that can be done when there is free time available.

Responsibilities

- model desired behaviors

- dress appropriately

- respond only when the student needs assistance or the placement officer requires more detailed information

- have a clear understanding of the job and the workplace

- understand the goals and objectives to be met by the student in the work placement

- understand and assist in creating task analysis for the student

- report daily on student successes, quantity and quality of tasks, time spent completing tasks, number of cues required to complete tasks, areas requiring further training, self-help skills required, salutations and communication ease

- debrief with the student and designated teacher in an appropriate environment

- be prepared to videotape student in the workplace once required forms are completed.

Chapter Two

Self-awareness

The career planning process begins with an individual developing an awareness of self.

This chapter is designed to provide students with an opportunity to learn more about themselves. Teenagers in particular need information about their changing bodies, personal growth and development, social boundaries and personal safety. There are a number of personal safety courses available for parents and educators. We have provided another option in this book which will help students with special needs and developmental disabilities to understand the issues that surround personal and safety boundaries. The Personal Peak Safety Program provides students with a concrete visual representation that allows them to clearly see where individuals belong in their social network. It also provides information about the appropriate interactions that should take place with these individuals.

The Personal Peak Safety Program has been developed to help students:

- access a visual aid to define social boundaries

- increase personal autonomy

- enhance personal safety

- increase social understanding

- become empowered to be able to say "no"

- understand issues around sexuality

- clearly define "safe" people who are available in the different zones to support them

- establish safe areas in the community

- understand the importance of

    ◦ nutrition

    ◦ hygiene

      ○ dress

      ○ language and conversations.

The Personal Peak Safety Program (see pages 43–52) relies on visual supports to help students *see* and increase their understanding of their physical, emotional and social maturation. Language is abstract. When concepts are presented in lecture format, students with ASD and other developmental disabilities often miss or misinterpret the information that is being taught. Because this program encourages teachers and facilitators to use visual and interactive methods, students become engaged with the concepts. This program can help influence a student's ability to understand the rules surrounding social language.

Consider the experience that Sam encountered when he kept swearing on the playground. He had been sent to the office a number of times, where he was reprimanded and given consequences. However, when Sam went back out on the playground, he began to swear again. The situation was not being resolved. When the problem was referred to the teacher, she asked Sam and his para-professional to take out their Personal Peak Safety Charts. The teacher wrote the words Sam was expressing on the playground on a sheet of paper. She showed the paper to Sam and asked him to watch what effect the words would have on his para-professional. The teacher then placed the paper in the para-professional's Personal White Safety Zone, which designated her personal space. Unaware of what to expect, the para-professional opened the paper and registered obvious shock. She asked Sam if he would ever say such a thing to her. Sam was quite adamant that he would never say those words to her. That led to a discussion of how words, even though they are invisible, can penetrate and violate a person's personal space. Sam then understood why his words were getting him into trouble and he stopped using them. Printing his statement and placing it in the para-professional's White Zone demonstrated how Sam had invaded her personal space. This was later tested on some typical students and the results were the same. Some very powerful and interesting discussions ensued as students as young as age 10 and 11 were able to talk about how powerful words can be. The experience gave these students important insights into how they need to be prepared to counter some of the influences that are being used to control their lives.

Maintaining an up-to-date Personal Peak Safety Chart enhances a student's understanding of the role he or she can be expected to assume to help increase personal safety and independence. Classes benefit immensely if charts and the concepts they represent are created or reviewed at the beginning of each school year. The Personal Peak Safety Charts can then be referred to when problem-solving situations that come up on the job, in the coffee room, going to and returning from work, and interacting with friends. There are no limits to the opportunities this program can provide for increasing a student's personal safety as well as enhancing relationships.

This chapter focuses on developing an appreciation of each student's individuality. The activities encourage students to examine their interests, strengths, personality, and values as they relate to work and leisure.

It is the goal of this chapter to help students working through these topics to develop a more positive self-concept based on a realistic appraisal of their abilities and potential.

Topic 2.1: I'm special

Objective: Students will begin to recognize they are unique.

Procedure: Read the following poem. Discuss similarities and differences. Have students try to think of one attribute they have that makes them special.

I'm special. In all the world there's nobody like me.

Since the beginning of time, there has never been another person like me. Nobody has my smile. Nobody has my eyes, my nose, my hair, my voice. I'm special.

No one can be found who has my handwriting.

Nobody anywhere has my tastes – for food or music or art. No one sees things just as I do.

Throughout all of time, there's been no one who laughs like me, no one who cries like me. And what makes me laugh and cry will never provoke identical laughter and tears from anybody else, ever.

No one reacts to any situation just as I react. I'm special.

I'm the only one in all of creation who has my set of abilities. Oh, there will always be somebody who is better at one of the things I'm good at, but no one in the universe can reach the quality of my combination of talents, ideas, abilities and feelings. Like a room full of musical instruments, some may excel alone, but none can match the symphony sound when all are played together. I'm a symphony.

Through all of eternity no one will ever look, talk, walk, or think exactly the same as I do. I'm special. I'm rare.

And in rarity there is great value.

Because of my great rare value, I need not attempt to imitate others. I will accept – yes, celebrate – my differences.

I'm special. And I'm beginning to realize it's no accident that I'm special. I'm beginning to see that God made me special for a very special purpose. He must have a job for me that no one else can do as well as I. Out of all the billions of applicants, only one is qualified, only one has the combination of what it takes.

That one is me. Because…I'm special.

Anonymous
(Source: Saskatchewan Education 1999)

Topic 2.2: All about me

Objective: Students will create personal biographies using a variety of methods which will help them to see changes they have experienced from kindergarten to the present. Students will learn to define their own individuality with the support of family and peers.

Procedure: Have students complete Worksheet 2.2A. Completing the enclosure will help them see how they have changed from being a child to becoming an adolescent. Encourage students to bring photos of themselves when they were about five, as well as a recent photo. They may access images via the computer or from magazines to demonstrate the answers for the other boxes on the chart. If there is access to a digital camera, students may wish to take photos that they can import or paste on to the chart. Send a copy of the assignment home to parents ahead of time, if possible, so that students can find photos or photocopy the photos to illustrate their projects.

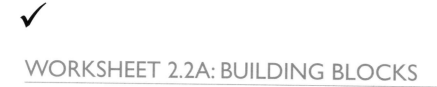

WORKSHEET 2.2A: BUILDING BLOCKS

The way I was and the way I am now

Me (paste a picture of the way you looked in kindergarten and the way you look now in the box in the correct column)	Kindergarten	Now
1. My height/weight		
2. My clothes		
3. My best friends		
4. My home		
5. My favorite TV shows		
6. My favorite games		
7. My most prized possession		
8. My feelings about • school • the opposite sex • telling the truth • being with my parents		
9. What makes me laugh		
10. What scares me		
11. What occupation did/do I want when I finish school?		
12. What school did/do I attend?		

Topic 2.3: Peer perspective

Objective: Peers will recognize and offer constructive comments about each other.

Materials: Large piece of chart paper, recent photo of each individual, glue, different colored marking pens.

Procedure: This activity can be completed with the assistance of the group. Place a recent photograph of the student on a piece of chart paper and encourage peers to make positive comments about the strengths, talents and observations they recognize in the individual. It is difficult for an individual student to recognize all the talents and qualities that he or she has to offer to the community. A well directed lesson can elicit some interesting perspectives from peers. Record all positive comments on the chart paper. Comments can include how the student:

- dresses (style)

- greets a friend

- helps out

- performs tasks

- participates in social groups or team sports in or out of school

- gets jobs done at home

- manages extra curricular activities

- initiates phoning others to organize outings or invite friends over to the house and what that entails.

Tease out any strengths, talents and unique characteristics the student demonstrates and explain how these can be very important assets in the wider community and in the workplace.

Record the information on a separate sheet so the student gets to keep a copy. If you have someone who can type and you have access to a computer as you do this exercise, have him or her record the information as the students are sharing their insights.

Topic 2.4: With a little help from my friends

Objective: Students will learn to recognize individuals who support them. They will define the areas in their community where they have responsibilities and participate in socially. They will create a collage representing this.

Materials: Photos, glue, two pieces of plain paper for photos, and/or two sheets of lined paper.

Procedure: In order to be successful, every individual requires a network of people and places that will support him or her. These include: family, friends, acquaintances and support personnel, as well as coaches and sponsors involved in the activities the students engage in at school and in their communities. Using one color of marker, have the class make a web of the people who can make things happen for them in their search for a full life. With a different colored marker, make a list of the places which will allow the students to access support and further training opportunities.

Discuss the possibility of taking photos of those individuals who are available to support students in the community. Think about the people who know the students and who are a part of their support network such as: bus drivers, swim coaches, lifeguards, individuals at community living centers, instructors for locally developed courses, and community college counselors. Encourage parents to provide photos of those individuals in the student's life who will be available in some capacity to encourage access to placement opportunities. This approach provides students with a more concrete understanding of who can help them maintain a rich and fulfilling life.

In addition, attempt to have pictures of places in the community which students will access as adults to help them maintain a balanced lifestyle. Consider including possible job sites and leisure sites such as: a theater, pool, shopping center, community hall, library, bowling alley, college, art gallery, and church.

Topic 2.5: Road map to today

Objective: Students will receive a visual map of the milestones they have met on their journey from birth to the present day. The road map will include all the successes students have experienced. Students will also be encouraged to include the challenges that they have encountered. A discussion about the importance of overcoming difficulties can provide students with an increased awareness of the need for effective problem-solving strategies. (More information about problem-solving techniques can be found in Chapter Four.) The milestones students have experienced can be discussed to demonstrate the skills they acquired as they met the milestones.

Procedure: Using Worksheet 2.5A for ideas, have the students create a dateline on Worksheet 2.5B. Have students record milestones on the dateline. Have students star the events that helped them to learn more about themselves. Worksheet 2.5C can be enhanced over time with assistance from home.

✓

WORKSHEET 2.5A: ROAD MAP TO TODAY

Map out your life like a journey through time with high points, low points, roadblocks, detours, etc.

At various points on your road map, note any event from which you learned something about yourself. Dates are important as they will help you to create your resumé at a later date.

Events to be noted on your map:

- clubs (Beavers, Scouts, Guides, etc.)
- athletic participation (in and out of school)
- training courses outside of school (first aid, babysitting)
- drama productions
- music events
- awards
- travel
- volunteer work and unpaid work experience
- paid work experience
- major family events
- school involvement (leadership, peer tutoring, T.A.)
- unusual activities
- moving
- births/deaths

Example

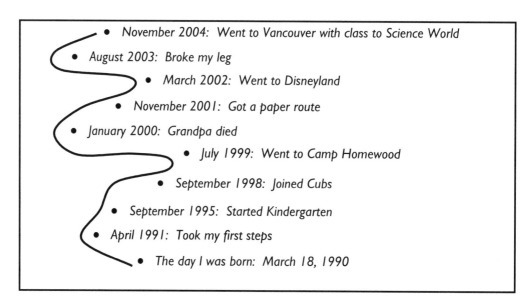

- November 2004: Went to Vancouver with class to Science World
- August 2003: Broke my leg
- March 2002: Went to Disneyland
- November 2001: Got a paper route
- January 2000: Grandpa died
- July 1999: Went to Camp Homewood
- September 1998: Joined Cubs
- September 1995: Started Kindergarten
- April 1991: Took my first steps
- The day I was born: March 18, 1990

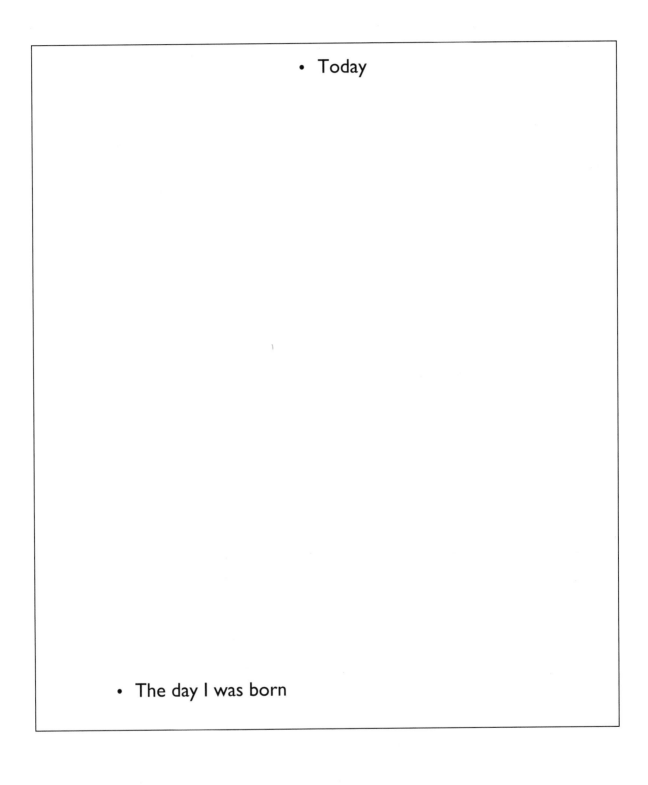

- Today

- The day I was born

WORKSHEET 2.5C: ROAD MAP

Take the information from your "Road map." On this chart, list the responsibilities you had, the frequency of your experience (how often), and the skills you required for this experience.

Responsibility	Frequency	Skills required
Example: Newspaper route	Every Wednesday	• being on time • collecting money

Topic 2.6: How to share information – a social skill

Objective: Students will create a visual representation of the highlights in their lives to share with others.

Procedure: Encourage students to prepare a scrapbook, PowerPoint slide show, or project that includes pictures, postcards, mementos and some written comments from others that describe events the student has experienced. Pictures and memorabilia can provide meaningful information for students with communication and organization difficulties. This approach encourages focused communication and can provide the student with necessary practice in sharing insights, information, answering questions and validating important moments in his or her life. For students who are nonverbal, a variety of technological approaches can be accessed to help a student communicate his or her ideas and insights. Set BC (the Special Education Technology of British Columbia) has a website that describes the various technologies available for those students who are nonverbal (www.setbc.org).

Topic 2.7: My strengths

Objective: Students will establish positive feelings toward self and others. They will identify personal strengths, interests and talents.

Procedure: Have students draw a circle in the middle of a piece of paper. Have them write their name or place a picture of themselves in the circle. Create smaller circles around the center circle and draw lines to the inner circle. Have students web their strengths in the smaller circles. Use the information the students have generated in previous exercises to encourage them to recognize the skills and abilities that have previously been reported. This exercise provides students with important insights about the types of work and leisure activities students may wish to pursue.

This assignment can be taken home to be shared with the family.

Topic 2.8: I know I can – my abilities

Objective: Students will refine their understanding of their skills and interests.

Procedure: Have students list all the things that they have recorded on Worksheet 2.8A: What can I do? Begin with the simplest of tasks and work into the more complex ones. It is important to remember that all aspects of the student's life need to be examined to insure that nothing is left out. When looking at what a student can do, don't forget to include self-help skills such as packing a lunch, washing clothes, taking the bus, using the phone, making beds, washing windows, vacuuming, getting around town, and shopping. These reflect a number of valuable skills.

Worksheet 2.8B: Machines I can use encourages students to create a list of every machine he or she has used successfully at home or in school. Anything that has a plug, switch, or motor can be listed, including mixers, blenders, sanders, and vacuum cleaners. For those students who have difficulty reading, try having them create a poster of all the machines they use. For some students, you may wish to make a photo journal that depicts them using the machine. Students may also be encouraged to describe in simple terms what they do with the machine. If, for example, a student uses a lawnmower, ask him or her to be specific about how often and for whom. This information can lead to an awareness of a responsible duty he or she can use on a resumé.

Have students complete Worksheet 2.8C: What I like to do. This will give them a better understanding of the environments and activities they may wish to pursue.

Have students complete Worksheet 2.8D: Putting my puzzle together. This will help them discover goals they may wish to strive to attain. It will also help them focus on the skills they will need to acquire to become successful in achieving these goals. This is an opportunity to encourage students to maintain realistic goals.

✓

Things I have tried
1.
2.
3.
4.
5.
6.
7.
8.
9.
10.
11.
12.
13.
14.
15.
16.
17.
18.

Machines I have used
1.
2.
3.
4.
5.
6.
7.
8.
9.
10.
11.
12.
13.
14.
15.
16.
17.
18.

WORKSHEET 2.8C: WHAT I LIKE TO DO

Put a check mark in the column which describes you best.

I like to	Often	Sometimes	Not often
1. Be outdoors			
2. Be indoors			
3. Draw			
4. Talk to people			
5. Work alone			
6. Work with my hands			
7. Try new things			
8. Help others			
9. Make people happy			
10. Collect things			
11. Read books			
12. Work with numbers			
13. Work with machines			
14.			
15.			
16.			
17.			
18.			

✔

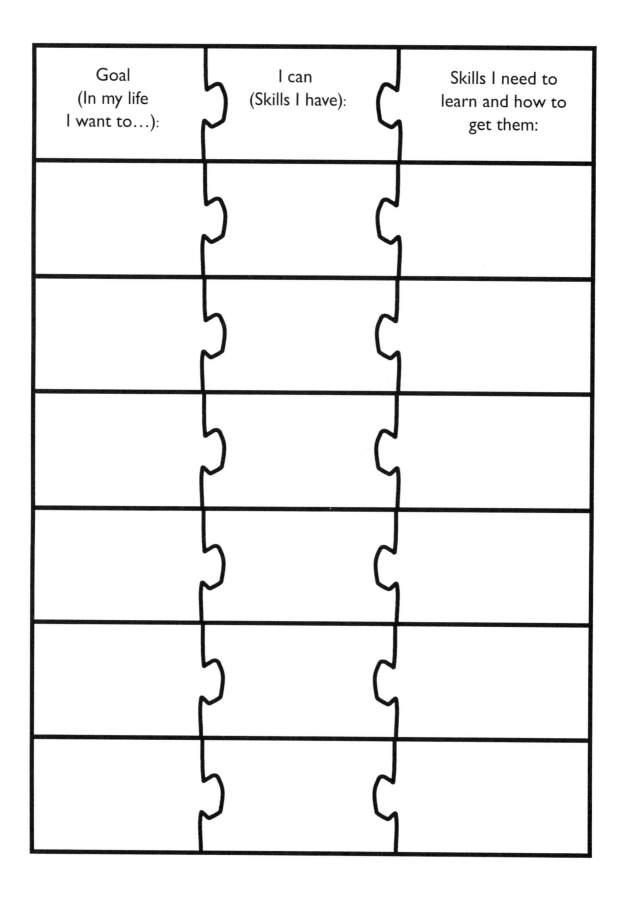

Goal (In my life I want to…):	I can (Skills I have):	Skills I need to learn and how to get them:

Topic 2.9: Increasing personal and sexual awareness: Personal Peak Safety Program

Objective: Students will become more aware of themselves personally and sexually. Students will increase socially appropriate behaviors. Students will increase personal safety skills.

This topic involves teaching students critical skills, and therefore requires formal teaching. A student's success in learning these important personal safety skills can be enhanced when everyone on a student's team understands and supports the skills students are learning. Parent/guardian permission forms should be filled out according to school district policies when teaching issues around sexuality. Personal and sexual awareness and safety concepts are dynamic topics that students may always require support understanding and applying. The environment for teaching this topic has to be one that promotes confidentiality and respect. There may be times when students encounter confusing experiences where personal safety may be an issue. Students will be introduced to the concepts of personal and private, appropriate personal space, as well as how to access *safe* people who can help them problem-solve the issues that arise. If students encounter difficulties or unexpected situations on a job site, these may be presented to the class, without reference to the particular student. Real experiences provide meaningful events that can become valuable lessons to help all students increase their awareness of situations that can become potentially embarrassing or dangerous. Using real experiences enables students to develop strategies they can implement if they find themselves in similar situations. Role-playing, Social Stories™ and comic strip conversations should all be used to enhance understanding.

Support personnel on the job site must be briefed so they can coach students and help them to generalize the skills they are learning. Remember to keep parents informed about the topics and strategies being taught so that everyone on the team can continue to support the individuals as they develop social and sexual maturity.

Procedure: In this section of the course, it is important to obtain real photos of the people who will be placed in the personal safety zones (see page 52) that are closest to the student. It is imperative that students learn to recognize and understand those who support, guide and protect them. As relationships become less familiar and more distant, such as in the last two or three zones, drawings or symbols may be used. Parents and/or guardians must be consulted to insure appropriate placement of the photos that are being used in the two zones closest to the student's personal zone, the White Zone. In addition, parents remain a vital link in helping to promote generalization of concepts across environments.

ACTIVITY 2.9A: PERSONAL PEAK SAFETY CHART

Many students with autism spectrum conditions do not understand personal boundaries. They require direct teaching and a visual means for comprehending these essential life skills. The Personal Peak Safety Chart provides a concrete means for helping students acquire and apply the rules that dictate personal awareness, personal space, boundaries and personal safety.

This approach recommends that the teacher guides students through the Personal Peak Safety Chart. A Personal Peak Safety Chart is an effective method to demonstrate to visual learners the dynamics that individuals find themselves faced with in everyday life. Students can learn how people in their lives may move across some zones but may never violate the peak zone. Each student can learn to appreciate that everyone has his or her own Personal Peak Safety Zones. Students will learn to clearly see their relationship to other people and the physical relationships these imply because students will use real photos and/or drawings or names to determine social boundaries. They will learn to apply social rules by relating to the different zones on the chart. This approach can be used with students of all ages.

In addition to creating a class chart, students will create their own posters that contain different zones on their chart. Each zone should have enough space to paste photos or drawings and/or name labels.

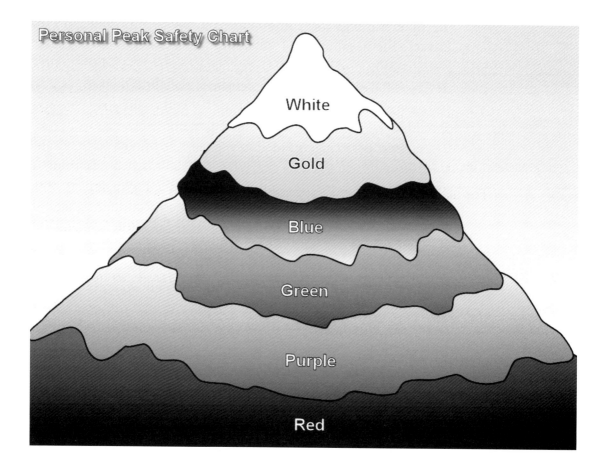

Step 1: Set the stage

It is imperative that the teacher establish a safe and trusting environment at all times. It is recommended that teachers meet with parents to explain the Personal Peak Safety Program and to discuss areas of concern that parents may have. Maintaining a collaborative partnership with parents helps insure important issues are explored, strategies are consistent and generalization across domains can be facilitated.

The ground rules that promote a secure and trusting relationship among the participants in the class need to be established at the very beginning of the course. Students must feel safe when sharing their experiences as they explore a variety of topics and debrief about some of the challenges they encounter at home, in the community, at school, and on the job.

Step 2: Create the backdrops

THE FLOOR MAT

The teacher is encouraged to create a floor mat to complement the Personal Peak Safety Chart each student fills in (Worksheet 2.9B, page 52). If canvas can be obtained, it may last for years, as long as participants who will stand on the mat remove their shoes before stepping onto it. Old sails are a very good source of material for these mats. If the teacher is in high school, the art department may be willing to help create the floor mat. Perhaps a parent volunteer may wish to design and make the mat. The peak itself should be big enough for an individual to stand in the White Zone securely and comfortably. The actual physical space from the peak or White Zone to the Blue Zone should be an arm's length away. This physical layout helps to provide a concrete experience of the normally accepted distance that people in most western countries consider socially acceptable.

PERSONAL PEAK SAFETY CHARTS

For making personal charts, the following options are available:

- Provide students with chart paper that has been pre-designed for them.

- Provide students with chart paper and a master so they can draw and color their own poster. *Avoid using crayons, as they will melt when laminated.*

- Give students clear guidelines for creating their own Personal Peak Safety Chart.

Supporting dynamic relationships

When the chart is complete, it is recommended that the charts be laminated. It is important to laminate the charts after coloring but before placing photos on the charts, as relationships change over time. Students will learn that while the teacher may begin the year as a relative stranger, in the Purple Zone, over time, as the student gets to know the teacher, he or she will probably move into the Green Zone. Classmates who have been in an outer zone may become more interested and involved with a peer and move to a more supportive zone like the Green or possibly the Blue Zone. Also, while most family members may be designated to the Gold Zone, there could be times when a brother or sister is designated to the far edge of the Purple Zone because of sibling conflicts. They can always move back when a conflict has been resolved. The importance of parent/guardian input becomes clear when a significant person who would normally be in close proximity to the White Zone is placed in the danger zone or is not present on the chart at all.

Defining the zones
THE WHITE ZONE IS THE PINNACLE OF THE MOUNTAIN

A picture of the individual creating the chart should be placed in the center of the White Zone. The picture will need to be updated over time, so be sure to paste it on top of the laminated surface. This zone represents a person's personal, private being. This White Zone can be described as a second skin that protects each person's individuality. Real skin protects us from disease, dirt and injury. Real skin helps keep our bodies intact. The White Zone helps us understand the importance of being aware of our bodies, our thoughts, ideals and culture. It is important to promote the idea that every single person is a separate individual who has a right to be respected and treated with dignity. This zone explores the concepts of personal and private in relation to one's body.

Facilitators need to make it very clear that no one should ever be able to enter the White Zone. This zone is sacred. It houses that person's uniqueness. This zone helps to define and conceptualize the meaning of personal boundaries. In a group situation, each individual clearly demonstrates with his or her own personal map, and by assuming control of the White Peak Zone on the floor mat, his or her own personal boundaries. It is a concrete approach that not only enhances an individual's personal understanding of the concept as it relates to him or herself, but allows each student the opportunity to see how others have private and personal boundaries, possessions, thoughts and rights. When teaching the concepts related to the White Safety Zone, the facilitator should use the term "personal space," or the term most commonly understood in the community.

When the students comprehend the physical boundaries this zone protects, the facilitator can expand discussions and lessons to include how possessions, thoughts, culture and rights are also private and personal. They too can be protected.

THE GOLD ZONE SURROUNDS THE PEAK

This zone represents those in the individual's life who treat him or her like gold. The people who would normally be put in this zone include those people who are the most significant people in the student's life: parents, brothers, sisters, partners, or perhaps a very close relative who assumes significant responsibilities for the child. They are the people who are permitted to hug and kiss them, take care of them when they are sick, and insure that they are safe and supported. The people chosen for this zone are keenly aware that an individual's White Safety Zone, "the peak," must be protected at all costs.

It is important that parents/guardians confirm who belongs in the Gold Zone. It should never be assumed that hired caregivers or babysitters belong in the Gold Zone, as many in these positions are often transient.

THE BLUE ZONE COMES NEXT IN THE SERIES

The people whose photos would be pasted in this zone are often close relatives, close family friends, and best buddies. Even though they may only see the individual occasionally, when they do they may greet them with a hug or a kiss on the cheek. They are important in the student's life but do not play the major role that those in the Gold Zone play.

THE GREEN ZONE SURROUNDS THE BLUE ZONE

The Green Zone includes people who associate with the individual in a positive, although more casual manner. Friends, peers, teachers, administrators, employers, colleagues, and support workers may fall into the Blue Zone.

The physical interactions used among different groups should be discussed, modeled and role-played. At this level, it is important to spend some time examining the types of interactions that a person has in the various community settings and with the different groups of people one meets. Students with ASD and developmental disabilities often lack an understanding of the roles that people hold. Consequently, being able to determine the difference between how one greets a police officer, an elderly lady and a peer may be something that the student has never learned.

Social greetings are determined by social groups. Where a student may use a fad greeting, such as a special handshake with a peer, he or she will need to learn the appropriate way to shake hands with an employer or a friend of the family. There is a lot of room for discussion and practice in this arena. Just remember that if you teach a greeting that is "in" today but may be "out" tomorrow, the child with autism or other developmental disabilities may not adjust to the change easily. Attempt to teach social acknowledgements such as nodding and smiling, shaking hands, and saying good morning, good afternoon and good evening. These are natural greetings. They cross all ages and social groups and have been around for a long time. Attempt to recognize the socially accepted interactions used in your community. When teaching students to shake hands, practice it! Greet students at the classroom door and shake their hand. The recommended handshake for greeting adults and employers is a firm, downward handshake that is not repeated. Eye contact, even if brief, can also be encouraged as a part of the process. As the teacher shakes hands with students, it will become obvious which students need to practice this simple but very important skill. Students can also shake hands as they leave the class and be prepared to make a positive statement on their way out.

THE PURPLE ZONE SURROUNDS THE GREEN ZONE

The people who fall into the Purple Zone are all those with whom the student would not have any physical contact whatsoever. We often think that this zone should be served for strangers; however, the concept of stranger is a very complex one. People we see regularly can be considered strangers in that we really don't know anything about them, other than the fact that they deliver the mail at a certain time every day, they stamp our books, or they sell us goods at a particular store. These people have designated roles. Outside of their work, we probably know very little about them. Are they married? Do they have big families? How old are they? Where were they born? Where do they live? What are their favorite foods/movies/colors? Have they ever traveled? There are a thousand answers the general public is not entitled to know.

The people who serve us in the community perform tasks they are hired to do. This can be a complicated concept for some students. However, it is vital that students begin to understand the relationships that exist between them and other individuals who are visible in the community.

People at the corner store, supermarkets and shops belong in the Purple Zone. Some students seem to think they know these individuals because they see them regularly and because they are friendly. Sometimes these are the people who talk to them the most. The facilitator needs to explain that the people are there because it is their job. The conversations they have are friendly conversations that usually only last a very short time. That is different from visiting. These individuals do not normally visit their customers at home, join them at dinner, celebrate birthdays or associate with them beyond the commercial setting. Isn't it interesting that in France, money is not exchanged from hand to hand but rather placed in a designated dish? A customer puts money in the dish and the clerk puts change in that dish for the customer to receive. There is no physical contact made between shopper and clerk. The relationship is clearly defined.

Students need to be able to recognize the professionals in the community who may be strangers but who are universally acknowledged as safe helpers. These individuals can usually be distinguished by the uniform they wear.

Although these individuals belong in the Purple Zone, they are considered safe strangers. They may be delineated by placing them on a light green background to illustrate that they are designated by the community to protect all the citizens in the community. They are there to keep people safe and healthy. The facilitator may wish to arrange for students to visit those places in the community where community helpers are available to assist them. If this is not possible, then the facilitator may wish to invite community helpers to come to the class and meet the students. When preparing to invite a police officer, health professional, cleric, fireman, or search and rescue professional, it is important to prepare the students for the visit.

- Watch a video, make a collage, and discuss the roles and responsibilities that the various professionals perform.

- Brainstorm with students about some of the types of experiences they may have had and generate a list of questions the students can ask.

- Consider assigning questions to individual students, so that as many students as possible get an opportunity to interact with that professional.

- Have students practice asking the questions they will be posing.

- Ask the professional to provide some basic information about the job they perform.

- Insure that the students know when and how they can contact the organization if they are in need of assistance.

When inviting visitors to the class, provide them with the information they will need to support a successful experience. If the class requires visual aids and demonstrations, ask your speakers to bring the required tools with them, so that their time spent in your classroom will be a meaningful experience for everyone.

Other people's children belong in the Purple Zone. Individuals with autism and developmental disabilities need to understand that they cannot pick up, cuddle or kiss other people's children. This can lead to serious repercussions as the individual gets older. It is safer to teach the appropriate actions right away in order to avoid what could be a heartbreaking and very confusing reaction from people who do not understand.

THE RED ZONE

The Red Zone contains real strangers, the people whom students have never met before. Review precautions that may need to be taken when individuals are approached by a stranger. Role-play allows students to practice how to react in the eventuality that they are approached by a stranger. Different scenes and potentially dangerous situations should be discussed in a mature manner. Often individuals with developmental disabilities can become overwrought if the situations are overly dramatized. In teaching these life skills, be prepared to model self-control as the students learn how to respond to uncomfortable or unusual requests. Practice, discuss and review them regularly. Encourage students to bring experiences to the class and share how they felt and how they responded. Remind them that social interactions are dynamic; they constantly change. Sometimes a situation a student has experienced numerous times may vary subtly. This can create confusion and anxiety in some students, because any change can make the entire experience appear new and unfamiliar.

Students will encounter a variety of situations in school, the community, the workplace, and the neighborhood that cause them concern. When a person is frightened or panics, the ability to rationally examine the situation can be severely compromised. Therefore, it remains important to continue to establish a time in the schedule that provides opportunities for individuals to share experiences. Validate their perceptions and attempt to help them clarify what they experience, so that they can describe a concern and create an action plan to respond to that concern. Create strategies that teach students to define what the real problem might be and then devise solutions that can address those problems. Develop a visual aid that helps them to "see" the problem and internalize solutions. There can never be enough practice and discussion about the ever changing social dynamics these students encounter. This is one area of learning that remains lifelong.

Safe people

As the Personal Peak Safety Charts are being created, it would be advisable for students, with assistance from parents and teachers, to recognize those individuals in their lives who are considered "safe people." A safe person is one who can assist the student when he or she is uncertain about what to do. Parents, principals, teachers, para-professionals, respite workers and special friends may be designated safe people. These individuals can be highlighted on the student's chart by pasting photos on a light green background before placing them on the chart. The photo may have a star beside it or some other visual marker that reminds the student that when they are confused or unsure, they can ask this person for assistance.

Unsafe people

Students occasionally encounter antagonistic or unsafe individuals who create stress and anxiety for the student with ASD or other developmental disabilities. While the situation is being addressed, a symbol such as a lightning bolt may be placed on the photo, or a drawing with the name of the person who is creating stress in the relationship. The lightning bolt can act as a reminder to the student with ASD or other developmental disabilities to either avoid that person or get a second opinion before acting on his or her suggestions.

Safety topics

In addition to discussing personal boundaries, safety and relationships, you can use the personal safety zones to address hygiene, appropriate dress codes, work safety, topics of discussion, speaking, writing, listening and looking manners, to name a few. In the workplace, students have to become aware that personal space also includes telephone conversations and private conversations. Visual intrusion is another area that we must remember to teach students, as staring at and observing private matters can cause discomfort for those who are working or attempting to deal with customers.

The way we dress, practice personal hygiene, play our music, listen in on others' conversations, and communicate by e-mail can all be addressed on the chart to help explain why it is important to respect others' personal cultures and values. These examples can be role-played and related to the workplace. All of these topics can dramatically influence an individual's success, both in the workplace and in relationships.

A facilitator can always refer back to the Personal Peak Safety Chart to reinforce social expectations. This is a valuable resource for explaining what the typical person in the community takes for granted. Support this approach with Social Stories™, comic strip conversations (Gray 1999), visual supports, role-playing, videos and situation specific examples to help promote greater and safer social mobility for students.

WORKSHEET 2.9B: PERSONAL PEAK SAFETY CHART

White

Gold

Blue

Green

Purple

Red

Topic 2.10: Emotions

Objective: Students will learn to increase their awareness of emotions in others as well as express their emotions appropriately on the job site.

Procedure:
1. Hand out "Feelings" (Worksheet 2.10A). Have students role-play the emotions that are reflected in the different faces. Explain how important body language is in communication.

2. Use a digital camera to capture emotions as expressed by the students. Arrange to print the images and have students paste them on playing cards, and laminate them.

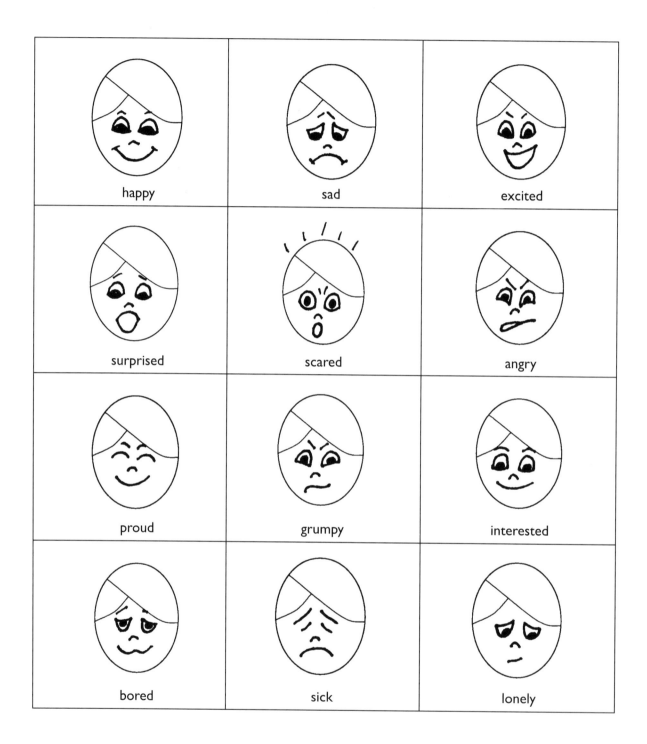

happy	sad	excited
surprised	scared	angry
proud	grumpy	interested
bored	sick	lonely

ACTIVITY 2.10B: DIGITAL PHOTOS

It cannot be assumed that students can read the messages relayed by facial expressions. Too often we resort to commercial programs that provide photos of people whom the students will never meet. It may be important for some students to actually learn to look at the people in their own communities and begin to interpret the emotions that these individuals are displaying. See if it is possible to take pictures of the significant individuals who associate with the students. Explore how individuals look when they are happy, sad, thinking, upset, frustrated, tired, or confused. Discuss why people feel that way and what responses we may use in those situations. Discuss how students can approach an individual to check out their assumptions.

As you create photos of students in the group expressing different emotions, consider whether you should have one set that is labeled with the emotion and another set that is unlabeled, since some students may read the label without studying the expression. Games such as charades and variations of "Go Fish," "Old Maid" and "Concentration" can be played to encourage awareness and fun while learning how to interpret faces.

Debriefing situations the students encounter with individuals or the group can be very beneficial. When students are in a work placement, supervisors should be encouraged to contact the teacher if the students encounter a situation in which they may have misinterpreted a coffee room discussion or work incident. Role-playing helps the students learn to focus on the subtle clues that give important information about what is taking place. This can lead to designing problem-solving cards which students can take home and/or to the work site to review and so, possibly, to avoiding unpleasant or embarrassing reoccurrences.

ACTIVITY 2.10C: EMOTIONS CHECK

In his book *Asperger's Syndrome: A guide for parents and professionals*, Tony Attwood (1998, p.91) proposes using a "barometer" that illustrates the intensity of emotions being experienced by an individual with ASD, in order to provide a visual and more concrete aspect to a very abstract concept. Students who have particular interests such as wind velocity, weights or temperatures can design a visual aid that helps them to recognize the various intensities emotions can take. In our experience it is advisable for teachers, parents and support personnel also to create a visual aid that allows the individual with ASD to see how they might be feeling. As individuals with autism lack the ability to mindread, many encounter significant difficulties when trying to "read" other people's emotions. They may think that they are the cause of the emotions another person is experiencing and be affected by this. When everyone has a barometer, each person can indicate what emotion they are experiencing and explain why they are feeling that way. This helps to make students aware that people can be feeling different for a variety of reasons.

Students should have access to a personal "thermometer" that indicates the different levels of feelings they can experience from *a little* (frustrated, happy, sad) to *very* or *extremely*. The thermometers can have words, numbers or symbols that students can relate to when establishing to what degree they are experiencing a particular feeling. Visuals should be available for students to place either on the thermometer or on the top, with a way of indicating the degree of the emotion. The visuals may be real photos or more abstract line drawings if the students relate to these.

When students indicate that they are angry, attempt to determine what it is that is making them angry, as this tends to be a generic term that really represents a wide range of emotions: frustration, disappointment, anxiety, fear and confusion, to name a few. Providing them with the appropriate words helps students to become more sophisticated in establishing where a problem may lie. This can then lead into problem-solving techniques which are discussed in Chapter Four.

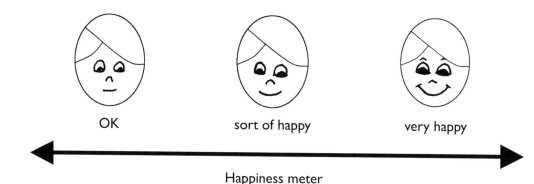

OK   sort of happy   very happy

Happiness meter

Chapter Three

Life Skills

This chapter builds on the earlier work on self-awareness. For the most part, students with ASD and other developmental disabilities receive extensive, appropriate life skills instruction from very capable teachers and support staff. The following suggestions and resources are meant to augment already existing programs, and by no means replace them. Life skills instruction assists students in their relations with other people: peers, adults, employers, friends, partners, parents, relatives, teachers, community workers, and all other people they may come in contact with throughout their lives. This chapter will focus on the more specific skills that relate to the challenges that students will face as they prepare to leave school and enter the world of work.

At some point during this unit, consider inviting guest speakers to the classroom to share their expertise with the students. Possible guest speakers might include: nutritionists, public health nurses, dental hygienists, estheticians, personal trainers, swim coaches, Special Olympic coaches, employers, and special education college teachers. These people will be able to demonstrate and discuss appropriate skills that could help enhance the students' health, lifestyles, work and social skills. Preparation before the guests arrive is recommended so that students can focus on the information that they will receive. Having a list of questions for students to ask can help facilitate connections between them and their guests. Invited speakers should receive an invitation well in advance and some speakers may need to be briefed about the audience: previous experience with the topic, level of understanding, and what types of visual supports might enhance the students' focus and understanding.

Many professionals come with a bag of show-and-tell items that the students can try. In some cases, such as the dental hygienist, he or she sometimes comes with toothbrushes or floss that the students get to take home. Once the teacher establishes a list of speakers, they can be selected to support the themes or topics that students are focusing on at the time. There often is not enough time to fit in all the speakers in one year, so teachers may plan to create a rotating schedule in which a guest comes every two or three years.

Topic 3.1: Personal hygiene

Objective: The students will be able to both explain and demonstrate that they understand the importance of age-appropriate personal hygiene and personal health maintenance.

Procedure: These skills are vital for successful job interviews, job placements and job maintenance. Students should have access to a full-length mirror.

- Activities 3.1A, 3.1B and 3.1C review the elements of good grooming and the necessity of using them.

- Teacher and students will discuss the importance of items on Worksheet 3.1D, "Appearing on the job," before a student goes for an interview.

ACTIVITY 3.1A: A PUBLIC APPEARANCE

Students must understand the importance of good grooming and physical appearance when they are going out into the community. They must be made aware that looking one's best definitely influences a successful interview. That first impression can make a significant difference as to whether or not the individual will be considered for the job. As a group, brainstorm how the students can prepare for an interview. The facilitator may want to distinguish between getting ready for a formal event versus a casual event. It will be important to emphasize that, regardless of what the event is, cleanliness significantly influences others' perceptions. This is also the time to discuss what clothing is appropriate for which events, as employers do not appreciate students showing up wearing inappropriate clothing for a job interview. Students can create a list or collage of appropriate clothing for job interviews.

Students should be encouraged to list the steps they need to take in order to venture out in public. Prioritize the steps that are essential for making a good impression, such as showering, washing and styling hair, using deodorant and putting on clean clothes. This may be an opportune time to discuss how to take a shower. (For those programs that provide opportunities to go swimming, insure that students know how to shower properly.)

ACTIVITY 3.1B: THE PARTS OF THE WHOLE

Maintaining good hygiene helps maintain good relations.

Discuss the possible problems that might affect one's getting or keeping a job. Discuss how to prevent problems and how to maintain a healthy and acceptable appearance. After all, the employer is not mandated to keep a person on staff if he or she does not meet the employer's standards.

Hair

Possible problems: dandruff, odor, style, color, length

Possible solutions: shampoos and conditioners (frequency); gels; brushes and combs; hairdressers/barbers

Skin

Possible problems:

Possible solutions:

Mouth and breath

Possible problems:

Possible solutions:

Feet

Possible problems:

Possible solutions:

Good posture

Possible problems:

Possible solutions:

Body odor

Possible problems:

Possible solutions:

ACTIVITY 3.1C: VERSATILITY

Create public appearance scenarios on index cards.

Include such events as:

- getting ready for a date

- going to Grandma's for Thanksgiving dinner

- preparing for a job interview

- mowing the lawn

- changing an oil filter

- going horseback riding

- going swimming

- going to a wedding

- attending a funeral.

Ask students to get into small groups and discuss how they prepare for the event they have been assigned. Ask them to choose one manner of getting ready. Let them know that they will be expected to present their preparation process to the class. They should be encouraged to write down and illustrate the steps using simple stick figures. If appropriate, they may be asked to role-play what they have prepared.

Collect the illustrated steps and post them around the class. Ask half the students to report on the differences they see in the different ways people prepare for different events. Ask the other half of the group to report on what similarities they see.

This provides the facilitator with an opportunity to heighten the awareness of people's emotional states during the different events, as well as the social rules that govern some of these events.

WORKSHEET 3.1D: APPEARING ON THE JOB

Name:	Yes	No
Is my hair washed and combed?		
Is my hair properly trimmed?		
Is my clothing neat and clean?		
Is my clothing appropriate?		
Is my shirt tucked in?		
Am I wearing a cap or hat?		
Should I wear cologne? (How much do I use?)		
Have I brushed my teeth?		
Is my breath fresh?		
Should I be chewing gum?		
Have I shaved today?		
Are my fingernails clean?		
Have I showered or bathed today?		
Is my jewelry appropriate?		
Am I wearing too much make-up?		
Are my shoes appropriate for the job?		
Are my shoes clean?		
Should I be wearing earrings or nose rings to this interview?		
Should I be smoking?		

Topic 3.2: Time management

Objective: The students will learn the importance of telling the correct time using analogue and digital clocks.

Procedure: Students should be encouraged to have their own watches and wear them regularly. Students should each have a daily agenda book that is used to record upcoming events and appointments. These should include school, work, medical and social appointments. Students should be responsible for getting themselves up each morning by using an alarm clock. Students can get used to filling out a daily timesheet (Worksheet 3.2A) to prepare them for that responsibility when they have a job.

Students can choose four occupations for their time charts from the list of occupations given on Worksheet 3.2B. Students should choose occupations of people with whom they have contact. Students interview a person who is involved in one of these occupations and obtain the necessary information to complete the chart on Worksheet 3.2C. Students' charts can be compiled to create a larger information base.

✓

WORKSHEET 3.2A: TIMESHEETS

Employee name: _____ Employee no.: _____ Pay period: _____			Total actual hours	Regular hours	Absent without pay	Illness	Vacation	Overtime	Other code	Reason
Day	Date	Shift hours Start / Finish								
Sun										
Mon										
Tue										
Wed										
Thurs										
Fri										
Sat										
Sun										
Mon										
Tue										
Wed										
Thurs										
Fri										
Sat										
Total hours										

Employee's signature   Supervisor's signature

Timesheets are to be completed daily and submitted to the office every second Friday.

✓

WORKSHEET 3.2B: LIST OF OCCUPATIONS

welder	grocery service clerk
tailor	newspaper carrier
artist	tile setter
machinist	painter
youth worker	office clerk
sign maker	fire fighter
excavator	gardener
hairdresser	electrician
childcare worker	baker
window washer	carpenter
meter reader	receptionist
computer technician	draftsperson
insulation installer	caterer
laundry worker	bus person
usher	lumberyard clerk
truck driver	gas station attendant
salesclerk	locksmith
ice cream vendor	packager
auto body worker	orderly
dish washer	nurse's aid
vehicle cleaner	bricklayer
mechanic	chambermaid
quilter	general farm worker
upholsterer	prep cook
veterinarian attendant	paper shredder
janitor	pet care worker
X-ray technician	

✓

WORKSHEET 3.2C: EMPLOYMENT INTERVIEW TIME CHART

TIME CHART	Occupation/ Job 1	Occupation/ Job 2	Occupation/ Job 3	Occupation/ Job 4
How many days a week do you work?				
What is your starting time?				
What is your finishing time?				
How many hours do you work a day?				
Do you do shift work?				
How long is your lunch break?				
When are your break times?				
What days do you have off?				
How many days do you have for vacation?				

Topic 3.3: Money management

Objective: Students will begin to learn the principles of budgeting.

Procedure: 1.   Students will obtain and manage a bank account.

2.   They should demonstrate the ability to use an automated teller card responsibly.

3.   They should be able to plan and budget their personal finances, whatever they are.

4.   They should know the real costs related to transportation, food, recreation, housing, and clothing.

In conjunction with their families, students should be involved with the above-mentioned expenses as they relate to themselves. Many students with special needs may also qualify for benefits or income supplements from the ministry that accommodates individuals with disabilities in their province/country. For example, in British Columbia, Canada, the Ministry of Social Services assists individuals in accessing financial support. Contact *your* local service agencies to request financial assistance.

Topic 3.4: Nutrition

Objective: Students will demonstrate and practice age-appropriate, healthy food choices.

Procedure: The students and teacher will discuss the importance of a healthy diet and how important this is in order for a person to be able to put in a "full day" on the job. Students should have the opportunity to shop for, prepare, and eat nutritious meals both at school and at home.

This is a topic that can be supported by a guest speaker such as a public health nurse, a nutritionist, a chef or a home economics teacher. The guest speaker may provide students with pamphlets and bring posters or video clips that help students recognize how important their diets are in supporting success in daily activities and work.

Your local public health unit should be able to give you information on healthy eating. You can find information and teaching resources about food online. For example:

- The BC Dairy Foundation at www.bcdairyfoundation.ca (Canada)

- The School Milk Project at www.schoolmilk.co.uk/ (UK)

- The Food and Nutrition Resources Information Center at www.nal.usda.gov/fnic/educators.html (USA)

- The UK Health and Well Being site at www.direct.gov.uk/ HealthAndWellBeing/fs/en

- Information on the Canada Food Rules at www.hc-sc.gc.ca/fn-an/food-guide-aliment/index_e.html

Topic 3.5: Community awareness and access

Objective: Students need to recognize and understand signs in and around their school and community. Students will plan and participate in regular trips to their communities to become aware of and comfortable accessing locations such as: theaters, libraries, recreation centers, shops, police stations, fire stations, hospitals, clinics, community centers, learning centers, courthouse, post offices, employment centers, ministry or state offices and other relevant resources.

Procedure: Students should be encouraged to walk as much as possible in their communities. Walking encourages a healthy lifestyle. In addition, it provides a valuable opportunity to help increase observation skills. Many students with autism and other developmental disabilities may not be picking up important cues that are available to them in their environment. Actively pointing these environmental cues out to students and questioning them about them are critical components that lead to increased independence, community mobility and good safety habits. It is essential that students become aware of signs in their community: street signs, logos, safety signs and block parent signs (see page 17). They may also require direct teaching to recognize and locate bus stops, routes, timelines and schedules. All students should be aware of the transportation services available in the community. Students should also experience opportunities to visit and use the various methods of transportation. Lessons on access and use of local transportation can enhance students' awareness of the roles that those working in the transportation field perform. Facilitating student access can also help establish community support as those involved become acquainted with the students. A collaborative approach can benefit both those learning to use the systems and those who run the systems.

ACTIVITY 3.5A: SCHOOL SIGNAGE

Access a variety of signs students would encounter in and around the school. Include all signs in the building, on the building, leading up to the building, and around the building including the parking lots and sidewalk areas. If your school is in a neighborhood setting, be sure to include street signs, as many students have not been taught to locate and recognize these important signs.

Some signs are commercially available. However, if you do not have access to any, consider asking a peer tutor, computer or media student or teacher, parent volunteer, or even students in the class, to go out with a digital camera to complete an inventory of the areas.

Using a digital camera allows a number of options for creating lessons:

- Cards with symbols can be printed and matching word cards can be created.

- Sets of cards can be made and students can use them in a variety of game formats.

- Students can be encouraged to discuss the importance of signs in their everyday lives.

- Students may recognize places in the school where signs are lacking and could be beneficial to others in the environment.

ACTIVITY 3.5B: COMMUNITY SIGNAGE

Acquire signs that normally appear in and around the community. Commercially available signs include functional signs. However, as in the previous lesson, the teacher may wish to lead the class on some environmental walks to help students locate and take pictures of the various signs in the community. If there are enough adults to supervise and accompany the students, the teacher may wish to allocate different zones of the town or city so that a variety of areas can be covered: the commercial zone, business area, factory area, residential areas, and shopping centers. The students could then compare signs and learn how to identify and respond when they recognize them.

This lesson can become even more specific with the support of businesses and managers in the community. Students can be encouraged to make appointments with persons in charge of theaters, libraries, churches, pools, arenas and auditoriums they frequent, in order to collect photos of the signs they should recognize and understand in the community. Students may want to create lists and compare them to determine the most frequently appearing signs. They might agree to set up learning stations to share their findings with other students.

1. Divide students into pairs and ask each pair to make a particular sign for display in the classroom. Students will need colored paper and/or feltpens.

2. Students set up a display area for their sign and are prepared to explore its meaning.

3. Students should be encouraged to create signs that inform, command, or warn people.

Suggestions to students could include:

> Restricted area
> Authorized personnel only
> Handicapped parking only
> Exit
> Help wanted
> Employees only
> Smoking prohibited
> High voltage
> Flammable
> Explosives
> Fire extinguisher

ACTIVITY 3.5C: GETTING AROUND TOWN

Students should learn how to access public transportation schedules in their community. They should learn where they can get the information, how to plan a route and which means of transportation they should access when there are choices.

1. Prepare a list of transportation options available to students in the region. For some students this may include reliance on family and friends, but the exercise of understanding that other people may have timelines and commitments needs to be discussed, as it can alert students to the need for advance planning with the persons involved. Help students learn how and where to access timetables. Do they need to go to the depot? Are there schedules posted in specific buildings in the area? Can they access the information on a website? If the student is able to drive or is asking someone else to take them to a new location, can driving instructions be found on MapQuest? (MapQuest is an online service for finding driving directions.) Do they need to phone ahead and ask for a map or directions?

2. Insure that students understand how to differentiate between the options available to them. Have them create comparison charts for distance, time and costs. Using real photographs as references helps students focus on the specific topic that is being discussed: type of transportation, places where they access the transportation, and places where they can access the information.

3. Once students become familiar with the process, plan an itinerary. If time permits, choose one of the itineraries and follow the plan. Take along a camera and continue to gather information. Follow up with a debriefing session. This can provide students with the opportunity to address any questions, anxieties or problems they may have, or think they might have, when taking public transportation. Create some of the experiences they might experience. Encourage the group to brainstorm solutions. Use a problem-solving chart such as a T-chart (see page 94) to help students define what may be a problem. Lead them through the process of defining solutions. Role-play the scenes so students actually get to practice the solutions.

Topic 3.6: The positive approach

Objective: Students will become aware of constructive criticism versus negative comments.

Procedure: In a social or work environment, people with positive attitudes are valued. Students with autism and other developmental disabilities may require direct teaching to begin to recognize what is a positive statement and what one might consider a put-down. The class is empowered when everyone knows the rule of thumb. That is, only thumbs-up are allowed in the class. Thumbs-down are definitely discouraged.

When encouraging positive supports among the students, use phrases such as "Is there a better way to say that?" or "Let's say that in a way that makes a person feel OK." This is a topic that cannot be covered in one class. It should remain an ongoing part of the curriculum.

When teaching students the concept of giving and receiving compliments, begin by asking each student to express a positive statement about another person. This trains students to look for positive attributes in another person. In the beginning, students may focus on the obvious, such as what someone is wearing. It is the teacher's job to develop an understanding of how people can be complimented on their actions as well as their looks.

It will also be important to begin to teach the students to think about others in their lives and how they support them. Get them to think about how Mom makes dinner every night. Does the family say thank you? How many times does Dad drive them someplace? How often does Grandma have cookies when they come to visit? How has the employer encouraged the success of their work experience? Have they said "thank you"? It is really important to foster a sense of appreciation in students. When the complimented begin to compliment others, people tend to stop and pay attention. When others stop and pay attention, this provides opportunities to enhance communication and social skills.

Practice this skill regularly until it becomes natural!

Topic 3.7: Conversation skills

Objective: Students will improve their conversation skills in order to become a member of the workforce. Conversation skills require an understanding of the different vocabulary and interactions that may be required among different social and cultural groups.

Procedure: 1.   Students will practice carrying on conversations with peers, teachers, parents, administrators, coaches, friends, employers and fellow employees, community workers and healthcare professionals. Provide a variety of opportunities for students to practice these skills throughout their school career.

2.   As a class, have students work through "What to talk about" (Worksheet 3.7A). This assignment can also be worked on at home.

3.   After handing out "Time to talk" (Worksheet 3.7B), discuss and complete as a class.

4.   After handing out "Body talk" (Worksheet 3.7C), discuss and complete as a class.

WORKSHEET 3.7A: WHAT TO TALK ABOUT

When getting to know people, talk about things that interest you – such as music, TV shows and sports. To help you in the future, complete the following statements:

The TV shows I like to watch are:	The sports I like to play are:
The movies I've just seen are:	The sports I like to watch are:
The music I like best is:	The hobbies I have are:
The food I like to eat best is:	The books I like to read are:
The animals I like the best are:	The places I have been are:

✓

A good way to start a conversation is to ask someone about his or her interests.

Use questions to start and maintain a conversation.

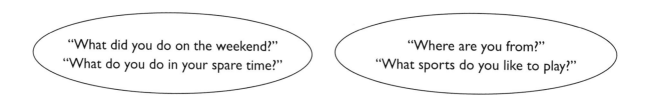

"What did you do on the weekend?"
"What do you do in your spare time?"

"Where are you from?"
"What sports do you like to play?"

You help a conversation by doing these things:

- giving others a chance to talk
- listening closely to others
- commenting on what they say
- being polite when you disagree
- learning to recognize when your partner is ready to end the conversation.

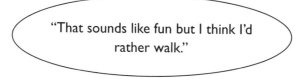

"That sounds like fun but I think I'd rather walk."

Time to talk

1. Discuss these questions:

   - Why is it hard to start a conversation with people you don't know well?

   - What might make having a conversation easier?

   - Think of different questions you can use to begin a conversation.

   - How does your partner know you are being an active listener?

2. Meet with a partner. Take turns pretending you are new to the neighborhood or new to a class. Have one person begin a conversation. Practice the questions you have created. Listen carefully to your partner's answers. Try to think of a comment that will keep the conversation going. Practice these skills with friends and family.

Friendly talk

Before and after class, or whenever talking is permitted, try to start a conversation with a peer. Try to remember to make positive comments or ask questions that are polite and friendly. Notice that the more you practice, the easier it gets.

Note: This can be a very difficult skill for people who have not had a lot of practice having conversations. It is also difficult when a person has not thought about the type of questions or comments that people like to hear. It may be important to practice this skill regularly until students begin to demonstrate the ability to initiate conversations with familiar people comfortably.

✓

Your face and eyes tell
a lot about how you feel.

Making eye contact with your listeners helps
to hold their attention.

Making eye contact when you are listening
shows that you are interested.

Your posture tells a lot about how interested
and confident you are.

Some mannerisms
can be annoying.

Time to talk

Meet with a partner. Choose a topic from the list below. Try to make good eye contact. Look as confident as you can. When you are listening to others, try to look interested in what they are saying.

Interesting topics

1. The best place I've ever been.

2. The best food I ever ate.

3. The greatest gift I ever got.

4. What it's like to water-ski or snow-ski.

5. The most exciting game I ever saw.

6. (Add your own).

Topic 3.8: Telephone skills

Objective: Students will practice a wide range of telephone activities both at home and at school.

Procedure:

1. Have students prepare messages they might need to give over the phone.

2. Students should have regular assignments that require looking up phone numbers, phoning for information, phoning friends, giving messages, taking messages and making "dates."

3. Teach telephone safety skills, such as who students would engage in conversations with on the phone. Refer to the Personal Peak Safety Chart (see page 44). Brainstorm a list of questions they should not answer. Teach phrases they can use that would not indicate that they are home alone, such as: "She is busy at the moment, if you call right back, you can leave a message." "I am sorry he is unavailable."

4. The way you sound when speaking on the phone is very important. Have each student find a partner (preferably each partner having the use of a detached phone). After the teacher reviews "How do you sound?" (Worksheet 3.8A), partners should work together on "After the greeting" (Activity 3.8B).

5. Arrange with parents for students to call home and leave messages that they can retrieve when they get home. They can leave messages about assignments, upcoming activities or social events they would like to join on the weekend or after school. This is a helpful way for students who tend to forget to make sure they remember when they get home.

✓

What you say and *how you say it* are extremely important when talking, both on the phone and off the phone.

The way you answer the phone can make a person feel glad they called or sorry they called.

Most people say "hello" when they answer the phone. Remember to say it like you're glad that person phoned.

1. Try saying "hello" in these three different ways:

   • cheerful

   • bored

   • angry.

   Do you hear the difference?

   How do you think you usually sound when you answer the phone?

2. Get a partner to listen to your greeting. How do they think you sound?

3. Consider practicing on a tape recorder. It is helpful because it lets you hear the way you sound to others.

ACTIVITY 3.8B: AFTER THE GREETING

Divide the class into groups of four. Have pencils and paper for the person who will be calling and the person receiving the call. Have each student prepare a message to relay over the phone. (Remind students that in real situations, they may get an answering machine. They should remember to wait for the signal that tells them when it is time to talk.)

Have one student pretend to call one of the peers in their group. The other two will act as supports. One of the peers will insure the person calling:

- speaks directly into the mouthpiece so that he or she can be easily heard

- speaks loudly enough to be easily heard without shouting

- speaks clearly so that each word can be easily understood

- speaks in a natural, friendly, polite way.

The receiving party will write down the important parts of the message. His or her partner will insure that the receiver:

- asks the speaker to spell important information

- asks the speaker to please slow down if they are talking too quickly

- reads the information back to insure accuracy

- or, if the student is unable to take a message, asks the party to call back at the time the person can take the message

- or, asks the person to call right back and leave the message on the answering machine.

Chapter Four

Decision-making, Goal-setting and Problem-solving

Decision-making plays a key role in career planning. Students begin to understand that once they have set goals they can begin to make smart choices. By following a process, students begin to understand that decision-making is a skill of choosing from alternatives.

Topic 4.1: Decision-making

Objective: Students will be introduced to the idea that decision-making is a process.

Procedure: 1.   As a class, list students' most recent decisions and how those decisions were made.

2.   Some decisions require little thought; others are complicated and need more time to figure out. Provide a list of decisions to be made, and have the class categorize them as to the degree of difficulty. *For example:*

Decision	I (easy)	2	3	4 (hard)
Take a shower				
Try out for the school play				
Choose a new pet				
Help a friend				

3. Write "Choices and responsibility" on the board. Brainstorm situations which require responsible decision-making:

    - choice of friends

    - choice about smoking

    - choice of leisure activities.

4. Once a goal has been identified, have students brainstorm choices:

    - How could I spend $20?

    - What will I do for the summer?

Topic 4.2: Decisions made easy

Objective: To help students learn a model for decision-making.

Procedure: 1. Hand out the sample decision chart to each student (Worksheet 4.2A).

2. Review and complete Worksheet 4.2A as a group.

3. Complete Worksheet 4.2B in pairs.

4. Change partners and complete Worksheet 4.2C.

5. Hand out blank chart to each student. Give all students the same general question, i.e. "What will I get my mother for Mother's Day?" Have students fill in choices under "Alternatives" and "Criteria."

6. Students should be given several opportunities to practice this exercise (using a fresh chart each time).

General question: What will I do on Sunday night?

Answer: _____

	Alternatives (Choices)			
Criteria (I need to ask myself)	**A** Go to the teen center	**B** Go to the movies	**C** Do my homework	**D** Babysit
1. Do I have parental permission?				
2. Do I have money for admission?				
3. What are my friends doing?				
4. What will I wear?				
5. Do I need to meet deadlines?				

✓

WORKSHEET 4.2B: DECISION CHART

*General question:*_____

Answer: _____

	Alternatives (Choices)			
Criteria (I need to ask myself)	**A**	**B**	**C**	**D**
1.				
2.				
3.				
4.				
5.				

WORKSHEET 4.2C: DECISION CHART

Question: _____

Sample

	My choices are			
I need to ask myself	**A**	**B**	**C**	**D**
1.				
2.				
3.				
4.				
5.				

Question: Should I lend money to a friend?

	My choices are			
I need to ask myself	*Say no*	*Buy it for him/her*	*Walk away*	*Say I have no money*
1. Can I afford it?				
2. Will I get it back?				
3. Is this a real friend?				
4. Am I allowed?				

Question: Should I buy a pet?

	My choices are		
I need to ask myself	*Visit animal shelter*	*Animal sit*	*Not have pet*
1. Am I allowed?			
2. Do I have allergies?			
3. Do I have money for food?			
4. Do I have money for a vet?			
5. Do I have time for an animal?			
6. Do I have space for an animal?			

Topic 4.3: Setting goals

Objective: To show students the importance of setting short- and long-term goals.

Procedure: 1.   Teacher discusses with the group the following terms:

- *goal* – something you want and can work to achieve

- *realistic goal* – getting a job vs. winning the lottery

- *short-term goal* – can be achieved quickly (seeing a new movie)

- *long-term goal* – takes time and planning (becoming a teacher).

2.   Using chart paper or blackboard, divide into two headings: "Long-term" and "Short-term." Have students generate goals and decide where each belongs. Put "R" beside realistic goals and "U" beside unrealistic goals.

3.   Have students complete Worksheet 4.3A (Decision chart).

WORKSHEET 4.3A: DECISION CHART

Directions: Make a list of goals under each heading below. Then choose **one** short-term goal and **one** long-term goal.

What do I want?

My short-term goals	My long-term goals

The **short-term goal** I have chosen is:

The steps I will take to achieve this goal are:

1.

2.

3.

The **long-term goal** I have chosen is:

The steps I will take to achieve this goal are:

1.

2.

3.

The steps I still need to take are:

1.

2.

3.

Topic 4.4: Achieving goals

Objective: To show students the importance of setting short- and long-term goals.

Procedure: 1.   Teacher discusses "Achieving goals" with students (Activity 4.4A).

            2.   Students choose a partner and complete "Your goals" (Worksheet 4.4B).

ACTIVITY 4.4A: ACHIEVING GOALS

The purpose of this exercise is to help students plan how to achieve their goals and to introduce the concept of setting realistic goals in life.

Directions

1. Have students understand the necessity of a student/day planner.

2. Point out that in order to achieve a goal, people have to follow a plan of action. This involves good planning.

3. Review with the students the process of achieving goals.

   - Discuss how to establish a plan to achieve a goal.

   - Ask students to share tips on how they have achieved goals.

   - Go over these conditions for setting goals:

     C harted – chart and measure the goal as you work to achieve it.

     L ogical – describe the goal in precise terms.

     E fficient – define a given time frame in which the goal can be completed.

     A chievable – be sure the goal is one that can really happen.

     R ealistic – think about opportunities that you can control in order to make the goal successful.

Goals

4. Ask students to work with a partner on Part I of Worksheet 4.4B. Encourage discussion. Any goals that do not satisfy the five conditions should be rewritten.

5. Ask students to change partners and complete Part II.

6. With the entire class, ask students to verbally commit to one goal. Set a timeframe for each student's goal. Encourage class members to help that person plan what needs to be done to achieve the goal and to help to evaluate the success or failure of the plan.

7. This activity should be repeated as regularly as possible so that students become accustomed to automatically noting their goals.

✓

WORKSHEET 4.4B: YOUR GOALS

Part I: Your goals

Write three goals you want to accomplish *today*:

Example: Get my math homework finished.

Steps to take:

1. Make sure I understand the assignment.

2. Ask teacher for help if I don't.

3. Set time aside to do homework.

4. Make certain I am not disturbed.

My goals for today are:	I need to:

Now write your goals according to order of importance, with 1 as the most important and 3 as the least important.

1. _____

2. _____

3. _____

Write three goals you want to accomplish *this week*:

Example: Go to the movies with a friend Saturday afternoon.

Steps to take:

1. Am I free to go?

2. Call a friend to go with me.

3. Have enough money.

4. Have a way to get there and back.

My goals for this week are:	I need to:

Now write your goals according to order of importance, with 1 as the most important and 3 as the least important.

1. _____

2. _____

3. _____

Write three goals you want to accomplish *this month*:

Example: Go swimming four times.

Steps to take:

1. Mark my goal on the calendar.

2. Go with a friend.

3. Give myself a star each time I go.

My goals for this month are:	I need to:

Now write your goals according to order of importance, with 1 as the most important and 3 as the least important.

1. _____

2. _____

3. _____

Part II: Sharing your goals

1. **C** How will you know you have reached your goal?

2. **L** Is it clearly stated? Do you know exactly what you are trying to do?

3. **E** What is your starting time? When will you finish? Will you be on time?

4. **A** Is this goal possible for you to accomplish?

5. **R** Have you created a plan to get it done?

Part III: Reflecting on your goals

After this discussion with your partner, feel free to modify your goals. Verify that your goals meet all five criteria for "Clear goals."

Topic 4.5: Problem-solving

Objective: To provide students with a visual approach to problem-solving.

Procedure: Draw a T on the board or chart paper. Define the problem. Under the T divide the area into columns. Label each column. Brainstorm with students for their interpretation of the label. When this is complete, create a chart that indicates the choices students have for solving the problem on one side of the chart, and the possible consequences of their choices on the other side. Discuss the difference between good choices and bad choices. Encourage students to try to make good choices. See the following example for ideas generated by one Career Training and Personal Planning class.

PROBLEM: Teasing

Looks and sounds like	Feels like
intimidation	empty stomach
mad/angry	broken heart
mocking	sad
name-calling	hurt
rumors	embarrassed
dumb jokes	crushed
dumb actions	an outsider
bossiness	
they are better than you are	

SOLUTIONS

Looks and sounds like	Feels like
walk away	stops but not always
ignore	stops
tell a *safe person*	stops and they can make you feel better, he or she can help devise a plan
punch them	more trouble or could stop
tell them to stop	stop or not
go to a safe place	stop

WORKSHEET 4.5A: WHAT IS MY PROBLEM?

PROBLEM

Looks and sounds like	Feels like

SOLUTIONS

Looks and sounds like	Feels like

Chapter Five

Career Awareness

This chapter explores career opportunities and requirements. For many special students, this awareness will be a critical factor when considering their career development. They must become more aware of realistic opportunities that exist for them in the world of work and begin to identify with the role of the worker.

One of the primary objectives of this theme is to expand the students' knowledge of potential occupations they may wish to pursue. It is hoped that students will also begin to understand how occupations can be categorized. Finally, this topic attempts to provide students with the job search skills necessary to obtain employment.

Topic 5.1: A–Z

Objective: Students will broaden their knowledge of occupations.

Procedure: 1.   The first student names an occupation beginning with the letter
                     "A" from a list posted in the classroom (see Activity 5.1A). The
                     next student then names an occupation beginning with the letter
                     "B" from the same list – and so on, until the alphabet is complete.

              2.   The game is repeated, but this time students must suggest
                     occupations without looking at the list.

              3.   Students must return to their next class with a list of the
                     occupations of the people in their neighborhood.

ACTIVITY 5.1A: LIST OF OCCUPATIONS

welder

machinist

excavator

window washer

insulation installer

usher

salesclerk

auto body worker

vehicle cleaner

quilter

veterinarian attendant

X-ray technician

newspaper carrier

painter

firefighter

electrician

carpenter

draftsperson

bus person

gas station attendant

packager

nurse aid

chambermaid

prep cook

pet care worker

tailor

youth worker

hairdresser

meter reader

laundry worker

truck driver

icecream vendor

dish washer

mechanic

upholsterer

janitor

grocery service clerk

tile setter

zoo keeper

office clerk

gardener

baker

receptionist

kitchen helper

lumberyard clerk

locksmith

orderly

bricklayer

general farmworker

paper shredder

Topic 5.2: Community awareness

Objective: Students will become familiar with occupations in their community. In addition, students will become knowledgeable about occupations they may explore, aspects of the occupations and the skills required to succeed in them.

Procedure:

1. Create a web on an overhead, the board, or chart paper. In the center of the web, write: "Jobs in my world." Enlist a student to describe the first hour of a typical school day. As students begin to respond, bring their attention to the physical items that are a part of daily life, i.e. vehicles, media tools such as radio and TV, household products and food products that are a part of their environment. Prompt students with questions such as: "What wakes you in the morning?" If a student responds with "the radio," then ask what jobs are connected to the radio. Place "radio" on the web and create another web around it. List the jobs it takes to produce the radio and get it from the factory to a home. Then explore all the jobs that are involved in producing the radio programs the students listen to. This exercise can help make students aware that what appears as a simple object actually encompasses a multitude of contributing factors to get from the drawing board to the bedside table and produce sound.

2. Bring a box of cereal to the class. Ask students which jobs went into producing the product. List all the occupations, from farming to design, transportation, shelving and selling.

3. As a class, choose three occupations. Define occupation as "working alone" or "member of a team." Define all aspects of the occupation and determine the skills required. See the following example:

Occupation	Working conditions	Aspects of occupation	Skills requirements
Jeweler	Working alone	<ul><li>beads</li><li>minerals</li><li>tools</li><li>earrings</li></ul>	<ul><li>finish high school</li><li>be creative</li><li>steady hand</li><li>use tools</li><li>know materials</li></ul>
Waitress	Team member	<ul><li>wash dishes</li><li>wipe tables</li><li>be clean</li><li>good communicator</li></ul>	<ul><li>finish high school</li><li>be pleasant</li><li>good on your feet</li><li>enjoy people</li><li>smile</li></ul>
Housekeeper	Working alone	<ul><li>vacuuming</li><li>cleaning chemicals</li><li>equipment</li><li>perfection</li></ul>	<ul><li>finish high school</li><li>be a hard worker</li><li>neat</li><li>know what products to use</li><li>read labels</li><li>understand signs</li><li>know time</li></ul>

Topic 5.3: Occupational search

Objective: Students will learn how to research an occupation that is of interest to them.

Procedure: 1.   Students select one job to be researched, using Worksheet 5.3A. This job can be one seen on a film or during a field trip, etc.

                 2.   Discuss with the class the individual responses to this worksheet.

WORKSHEET 5.3A: CAREER WORKSHEET

Name: _____

This career study is on _____

1. On the job, my responsibilities would be:

2. The other tasks I may need to do are:

3. The environment is (noisy or quiet, indoors or outdoors, hot or cold):

4. Working conditions (seasonal, dangerous, standing or sitting, odd hours, tiring, heavy or light lifting, etc.):

5. Safety concerns:

6. Skills and aptitudes needed (academic, clerical, mechanical):

7. Physical demands (active or sitting, strength, height, weight, etc.):

8. Interest requirements (in machines, ideas, people, outdoors, etc.):

9. Education:

10. What I like and don't like about this job:

    Likes:

    Dislikes:

Topic 5.4: Occupational riddles

Objective: Students will learn to recognize occupations and associated attributes.

Procedure: 1.   Read the riddles (Activity 5.4A) to the students and have them name the occupation.

                        2.   Variation: students make up their own riddles.

ACTIVITY 5.4A: OCCUPATIONAL RIDDLES

1. My job is to cut down trees. I use a power saw and cut all the branches off the fallen trees. My job helps provide materials for building houses and furniture. Who am I? (*logger/faller*)

2. I make women beautiful by washing and styling their hair. Sometimes I color their hair and put in highlights. Who am I? (*hairdresser*)

3. I build sturdy houses and walls. I use a special kind of heavy block with cement in between. Who am I? (*bricklayer*)

4. I love to be out on the ocean in a boat. I work with a team. We put big nets into the water and catch fish. We sell fish to stores and markets for people to eat. Who am I? (*fisherman*)

5. You are glad to see me arrive at your door when you have a problem with your drains, pipes or toilet. Who am I? (*plumber*)

6. I work where it is dark and damp and dirty. I often go deep down into the earth where I chip and break minerals away from the sides of caves. Who am I? (*miner*)

7. I have to get up early in the morning. I bring news to many homes. Sometimes I use a bicycle to deliver my goods. Who am I? (*newspaper deliverer*)

8. I help people enjoy our national parks. I teach them how to play safely in the woods. Sometimes I take care of animals. Sometimes I become a fireman or policeman. Who am I? (*forest ranger*)

9. I pack and take the groceries to your car. I help find out how much an item costs when there is no price tag at the checkout counter. Who am I? (*grocery clerk*)

10. I place flowers into beautiful arrangements for churches, homes, hospitals, and for special occasions such as birthdays, anniversaries, weddings and funerals. Who am I? (*florist*)

11. I like to keep your car in good running condition. I change the oil, check the brakes, check the fluids and fix any parts that are wearing out or that are damaged. Who am I? (*mechanic*)

12. You come to me with your dirty laundry, drapes and sleeping bags. I wash and iron them for you. Who am I? (*laundry or dry cleaner*)

13. I can help you check your tire pressure or check your oil when you come to fill up with gas. You pay me when you have enough gas in your tank. Who am I? (*gas station attendant*)

14. I wear a uniform and cap. I use a bat and glove. I try to hit home runs. Who am I? (*baseball player*)

15. I work with gold and silver and beautiful things that are broken. I set beautiful stones and sell china, silver and crystal. Who am I? (*jeweler*)

16. I take orders and carry trays and serve all sorts of delicious foods. Who am I? (*waitress*)

17. I usually sit at a desk, answer phones, work on a computer, and file. Who am I? (*secretary*)

18. I love to work outdoors. I plant and sow, rake and hoe. I raise chickens, pigs, cows and horses. I have big machines that help me to do my work. Who am I? (*farmer*)

19. I entertain people by singing and playing music. I make CDs. I hold concerts and a lot of people come to hear me. Who am I? (*singer/musician*)

20. If a hailstorm made a hole in the top of your house, I would fit shingles together like a puzzle to cover the hole. Then you would be warm and dry again. Who am I? (*roofer*)

21. I wear a special kind of suit. My job takes me high into the sky. When I am at work, I can look down and see the earth. I float around my workplace. Who am I? (*astronaut*)

22. I stack cans on cans and boxes on boxes. I stamp numbers on the cans and boxes so that people will know how much to pay for them. Who am I? (*stock boy*)

23. Tap-tap-tap. I exchange old soles for new ones. I tack on heels and mend old toes and buff and brush and polish. Who am I? (*shoe repairman*)

24. I take care of little children when their moms and dads go to work. There are a lot of toys and games for the children to play with when the children are dropped off. The children learn nursery rhymes and listen to me read stories. Who am I? (*daycare worker*)

25. I love to work outside in the dirt. I make yards and parks beautiful. I plant lovely flowers and shrubs and keep the lawns cut. Who am I? (*gardener*)

26. I love the water and I watch people in pools to make sure that they are safe. I also teach water safety and swimming lessons. Who am I? (*lifeguard/swimming instructor*)

27. I drive a large vehicle all over town. I stop often to pick up passengers. When they need to get off, they ring the bell and I stop at the next stop. Who am I? (*bus driver*)

Now that the students have the idea, provide them with an index card. Ask them to think of a job. Have them list at least three attributes of the job they are thinking about. Inform them that they will be expected to share their description of the job they are thinking about with the class. The class will then try to guess what that job is. Remind students to be careful not to use the job word in their description. Demonstrate how to do the exercise, using an example.

Examples

1. I sort used bottles and cans.

2. I tie old newspapers together to be sent away and made new again.

3. My job helps save the planet.

   Who am I? (*recycler*)

1. I lead people out on the ocean; everyone has his or her own vessel.

2. I demonstrate how to steer a one-person boat with a long pole that has paddles on each end.

3. I teach people how to get back into their boat when they fall out.

4. Sometimes I take a group out on overnight trips along the coast.

   Who am I? (*kayak guide*)

Topic 5.5: Job ads

Objective: Students will become familiar with the classified section of the newspaper in order to access information.

Procedure: Access job ads from the classified section in a newspaper or refer to Worksheet 5.5A. Students will:

- pick a minimum of three jobs

- read the job descriptions

- write a description of the skills and abilities required to perform the jobs.

BINGO CALLER

Part time employment available at Campbell River Bingo. Help to have experience with a microphone. May require gaming registration. Apply in person with resumé:

Campbell River Bingo

151 St. Ann's Rd

or fax resumé:

250-286-0865

Attention Mike or Steve.

The WeWaiKai Nursery School/Daycare

has an opening for an Early Childhood Education (ECE) teacher. Position would be part time. Also looking for substitute ECE teachers. Applicants will need a current ECE license, current first aid ticket, and a valid BC driver's license. For further information please contact Pamela Lewis at 250-285-3316. Please fax resumé including references, copy of ECE license and first aid ticket to 285-2400, attention Pam Lewis.

LABOURER req'd for truck repair shop. Duties incl. yard maintenance and clean up. Apply with resumé to Alpine Truck and Equip. Repair, 960 Henry Eng Pl., fax 474-2023.

EXPERIENCED labourer or carpenter's helper. Truck or van required. Good wages, benefits, mileage. Apply Downs Construction, 870 Devonshire Rd.

PROF. Cleaning company looking for P/T reliable, exp'd cleaner w. car. Fem. pref'd. Leave msg 380-1396.

QUADRA convenience gas bar now adding to our team. F/T afternoons. Apply with resumé to 3790 Quadra St.

ESTHETICIAN part time position available in well established salon, Shawnigan Lake. Lois 250-743-5559.

EXP'D evening line cooks req'd by Smugglers Cove Pub. Good pay for the right person. Apply Mon–Fri, 2581 Penrhyn St.

SERVER

Part and full time
Julia's Place
609 Courtney St.,
Downtown

BUSY downtown hotel req's an exp'd P/T server. Flexible hours. Fax resumé 385-5800.

FT receptionist required for downtown law office, $10/hr. Duties include some light correspondence, multi line switchboard, filing, faxing, sorting mail, etc. Please drop off resumé in person to #203 – 919 Fort St.

Social Insurance Number (SIN)

To obtain a job in most countries, students must obtain a special card with a number on it. To access such a card students will need to provide original documents that verify their age, their identity and citizenship or lawful non-citizen status in order to obtain a job in that country. In Canada, this is called a Social Insurance Number (SIN). Contact www.hrsdc.gc.ca for information. In the UK it is called a National Insurance Number. Contact www.dwp.gov.uk/lifeevent/benefits/ni_number.asp. In the United States it is called a Social Security Number. Information can be obtained at www.socialsecurity.gov/online/ss-5.html. Following is an example of the procedure a student in Canada would follow.

Topic 5.6: Applying for a Social Insurance Number (SIN)

Objective: Students will learn the importance and value of having a Social Insurance Number. They will learn how to apply for one.

Procedure: Teachers can access SIN forms from their local government agent or online at www.hrsdc.gc.ca and follow the links.

1.   Teacher discusses general information about the SIN (Activity 5.6A).

2.   Provide students with two copies of the SIN form (obtained from the appropriate government office).

3.   Using an overhead transparency of this form, assist students in working through their practice copy.

4.   Students then transfer the information onto their "good" copy.

5.   Encourage the students to apply for a SIN.

ACTIVITY 5.6A: HOW TO APPLY FOR A SOCIAL INSURANCE NUMBER

1. How do you abbreviate "Social Insurance Number"?

2. Where do you apply for a SIN?

3. If you were born in British Columbia, what forms would you take to the government office? If you are a landed immigrant, what forms should you take?

4. What is an acceptable birth certificate?

5. What are four examples of other acceptable documents?

6. What do you have to do if you wish to register in a name that is different from the name on the document?

7. Is it best to apply by mail or in person?

8. What happens once your forms are completed?

9. What is the real purpose of a SIN?

10. When will employers need your SIN?

Topic 5.7: Application forms

Objective: Students will understand the meaning of words used on application forms.

Procedure: 1. Teach application form vocabulary given in Activity 5.7A.

2. Give students a number of opportunities to fill out application forms. Worksheet 5.7B is an example of a generic form. For further practice, access application forms from local businesses.

ACTIVITY 5.7A: APPLICATION FORM VOCABULARY

Social Insurance Number (SIN) – an identification number for each Canadian worker

National Insurance Number – an identification number for each worker in the UK

Social Security Number – an identification number for each worker in the USA

Surname or family name – your last name

Address – a way to identify your house

Marital status – single or married

Part-time – working less than 35 hours per week

Full-time – working 35–40 hours per week

Temporary – a job that lasts for a certain time only

Permanent – a job that you can keep as long as you want

Casual – similar to being on-call

Fringe benefits – payment in forms other than money (e.g. dental plan, pension plan, medical plan)

Days – working during daytime only

Evenings/afternoons – working usually between 3:00 p.m. and midnight

Graveyard or nights – working usually from 11:00 p.m. to 7:00 a.m.

Veterans preference – you have served in the Canadian Armed Forces

Minimum wage – the least amount you must be legally paid

Driver's license – the type of license to drive a car

Education:

- *academic* – courses like English and Math
- *trades* – courses you can take in the IE Department

- *commercial* – courses you can take in the Commerce Department such as typing and basic business

- *technical* – courses on computers and in graphic arts

References – names of people who would speak well of you

Duties – the things you are responsible for in a job

Position – the name of a job

Supervisor – your boss

West Coast Resources Limited
PO Box 1234
Campbell River, BC
V9W 5C1

For Office Use Only	
Name	
Position	Date

APPLICATION FOR EMPLOYMENT

Name First Middle Last	Social Insurance Number
Present Address	Postal Code/ZIP Code
Permanent Address	Postal Code/ZIP Code

Home Telephone Number	Business Telephone Number	Height	Weight
Birth Date	Marital Status	Number of Dependent Children	Age

Position Desired		Alternate Position Desired	
Salary/Pay Expected			Date Available
Type of employment desired Regular ☐ Temporary ☐	Will you accept shift work? Yes ☐ No ☐	Will you work weekends? Yes ☐ No ☐	May we contact your present employer? Yes ☐ No ☐

If applying for a CLERICAL position, complete the following:

Type speed	Shorthand speed	What business machines can you operate?
wpm	wpm	

IN CASE OF EMERGENCY, WHOM SHOULD WE NOTIFY? Name	Address
Relationship	Telephone Number

Have you applied previously to work for us? If so, when? Yes ☐ No ☐	Have you worked previously for us? If so, when? Yes ☐ No ☐
How did you learn of our company?	Names of friends or relatives working for us

Driver's License Number	Province/State Issued	Expiry Date	Country of Birth Landed Immigrant ☐
List any distinguishing physical features		List any recent illnesses	

Have you ever had a medical exam? If so, when?
Yes ☐   No ☐

Do you have a hearing defect?	Have you ever received worker's compensation? If so, give details Yes ☐ No ☐

✓

Education Name of Institution and City	Highest Level Achieved	Date completed
High/Secondary School		
Technical School (Apprenticeship)	Specialization	
University	Diploma/Degree	

Work History LIST EXPERIENCE STARTING WITH MOST RECENT EMPLOYER

FROM Month Year	TO Month Year	Name and Address of Employer	Position and Duties	Supervisor	Salary	Reason for Leaving

References DO NOT LIST RELATIVES

Name	Address and Telephone Number	Occupation
ADDITIONAL INFORMATION	List skills you have acquired, equipment and machines you can operate, valid certificates held, supervisory and teaching experience, and any information which will assist us to place you in a suitable employment.	

IT IS AGREED THAT PREVIOUS EMPLOYERS MAY BE CONTACTED UNLESS SPECIFICALLY NOTED TO THE CONTRARY ON THIS FORM. IT IS UNDERSTOOD THAT THE PASSING OF A PRE-EMPLOYMENT MEDICAL IS A CONDITION OF EMPLOYMENT AND ANY FUTURE RELATIONSHIP BETWEEN THE COMPANY AND THE UNDERSIGNED IS DEPENDENT UPON THE TRUTH OF THE STATEMENTS CONTAINED IN THIS APPLICATION. IT IS ALSO UNDERSTOOD THAT SHOULD I BE EMPLOYED, I WILL COMPLY WITH ALL COMPANY REGULATIONS.

_____   _____
          Signature   Date

Topic 5.8: Contacts

Objective: Students will recognize people and organizations in the community who might be of assistance when looking for employment.

Procedure: Teacher discusses the purpose of the following organizations:

- Local College
- Government Social Services
- Association for Community Living
- Human Resources Centers.

Topic 5.9: How to prepare a resumé

Objective: Students will learn the importance and use of a resumé. Students learn how to prepare a resumé.

Procedure: 1. Explain the purpose of including a resumé in one's job search.

2. Distribute Worksheet 5.9A or 5.9B (depending on level of students) and discuss. Clarify for students the type of information required in a resumé, and the various headings under which this information may be grouped.

3. Have students prepare their own resumé.

This Resumé Workbook Belongs to:

_____

How to start your resumé

1. Name:

   Address:

   Telephone no.:   Other phone no.:

2. Skills and interests:

3. List your most important skills or interests and what you have learned from them:

   a.

   b.

   c.

   d.

   e.

4. Work and volunteer experience:

   a.

   b.

   c.

   d.

   e.

5. Education (present school, grade, special courses):

6. Personal profile (things outside of school you like to do):

7. References (three people whom an employer could call; not family):

_____

(Name)   (Telephone number)

_____

(Name)   (Telephone number)

_____

(Name)   (Telephone number)

Resumé Workbook

How to write your resumé

HEADING

Include your full name, address and telephone number. Give an alternative telephone number to be sure the potential employer is able to get a hold of you. Do not include personal information such as your birth date, social insurance number, health, etc.

OBJECTIVE

If you are using your resumé for a specific purpose (e.g. to get a job at a store or in a particular area of work) write this down. If you are going to be using your resumé at a number of different places you do not have to include an objective. Ideally, you should have your resumé on a computer so that you can adjust your resumé for each job you apply for.

SKILLS AND AREAS OF KNOWLEDGE

This is the most important and often the most difficult part of the resumé. In as few words as possible, you must let the potential employer know what you are able to offer as an employee. Ask yourself the question "Why should the employer hire me?"

Skills can be classified in a number of ways, but to start with you must consider your recent experiences to discover the skills you have developed. Turn to the Skills Worksheet and complete.

WORK AND VOLUNTEER EXPERIENCE

Your work and volunteer experience (include teams you have played on if you wish) are always listed in order of the most recent to the oldest. Try to have four to five experiences, but don't let your list become too long. Do not include the oldest and least valuable experiences.

EDUCATION

Indicate your current grade.

SPECIALTY COURSES

Do not list all of your courses. Only list specialized programs you have taken such as first aid, babysitters course, swimming instructors program, etc. You may wish to attach a copy of your report card to your resumé.

ACHIEVEMENTS OR AWARDS (OPTIONAL SECTION)

This section can be anything special you wish to highlight such as a member of the volleyball team for five years, an exchange trip you might have taken, the best citizen of the school, etc.

INTERESTS

List four to five things outside of work and school that you enjoy, e.g. swimming, tennis, golf, rugby…

REFERENCES

List your references on the resumé to save the potential employer the trouble of having to call you for them. Include three – no more or less. Do not use any family member as a reference even if you have worked for that person. Use past employers, coaches, teachers, or people you have volunteered for. Include their full names, and their relationship to you (e.g. manager – McDonalds, babysitting employer, etc.), as well as their telephone numbers.

Sample resumé

Chris Parker
790 Marina Way
Campbell River, BC
V9W 5T8
923-9875 or 287-5483

OBJECTIVE:	TO OBTAIN SUMMER EMPLOYMENT.

SKILLS AND AREAS OF KNOWLEDGE:

Computer skills	Knowledge of WordPerfect 5.1, Microsoft Works, programming (Island Microsystems course), DOS. Type 40 WPM.
Hospital volunteer	Delivered water jugs to patients, ran errands for patients, served food, cleaned, kept patients company.
Soccer team	Developed responsibility, improved listening skills, developed hand–eye co-ordination, self-control and commitment. Learned the value of a positive attitude.
Paper carrier	Responsible for delivering newspapers and flyers to up to 100 homes on a bi-weekly basis. Accountable for money collected. Worked in the early morning and in all weather conditions.

WORK AND VOLUNTEER EXPERIENCE:

June 1994–present	Courier-Islander/The Wrap Paper carrier
Sept. 1994–present	Campbell River and District General Hospital Volunteer
1991–1994	Soccer team
EDUCATION:	Attending Southgate Secondary, Grade 9
SPECIALTY COURSES:	Babysitting course, 1991 Island Microsystems, programming course, 1994
AWARDS:	Citizenship Award, Grade 8
INTERESTS:	Soccer, baseball, swimming, tennis, reading (science fiction)

REFERENCES:

Albert Black Coach 287-9876	Mary Smith Hospital Supervisor 287-0198	Emma Simms Employer – babysitting 923-1948

✓

Skills and areas of knowledge

There are two kinds of skills: transferable and practical.

Transferable

These are skills which you have learned through a job, school, sports, etc. which are transferable to any job. These include such things as communication skills, organization skills, interpersonal skills, ability to follow instructions, customer relations.

Practical

These are things you can do such as operate a cash register, a computer, power tools, type 50 WPM, etc.

YOUR LIST

1. List all the experiences you have had up to the present.

   Examples:
   Played soccer or ??
   Took computer, food or wood courses ??
   Babysat
   Yard work
   Delivered papers
   Hospital or other volunteer work
   Group activity (cadets, scouts, church group or ??)
   Tutored
   Coached

2. Star the five you consider the most important (the ones you learned the most from).

3. Rewrite the five most important experiences and beside each write what you learned from the experience.

Examples:

Babysitting

Supervised three children aged four to nine, prepared meals, organized activities to entertain them, supervised their bedtime activities, learned responsibility and organizational skills.

Computer skills

Knowledge of programming, Word Perfect, Microsoft Works, desktop publishing, DOS; can type 40 WPM.

Communication skills

Good listener, able to understand and follow instructions, able to greet and communicate in a friendly way with customers, speak clearly on the telephone.

Insert your Skills and Areas of Knowledge paragraphs into your resumé. This section will change over time as you have more experiences and start working. Keep this up-to-date!

Topic 5.10: A job interview

Objective: Students will learn to respond to potential questions posed during a job interview.

Procedure:

1. Review Worksheet 5.10A (Interview etiquette). These tips should be practiced in the classroom regularly.

2. Distribute Worksheet 5.10B and have students write or verbally respond (depending on ability) to each of the questions posed by the interviewer.

3. Have students break up into threesomes and role-play the interviews. One person plays the boss, one plays the applicant for the job, and the third observes and rates the person applying for the job using Worksheet 5.10C. Students then switch roles.

4. Invite a volunteer familiar with local business expectations to visit the class and interview each student.

Helpful hints

- LOOK YOUR BEST. This is really important. Like it or not, the way you look will mean a lot to someone who is thinking about hiring you. Dress appropriately. If you are not sure what that means, ask.

- Show up a few minutes early. It will give you time to catch your breath and relax before the interview.

- Smoking cigarettes or chewing gum does not make a good impression.

- When you arrive for the interview, say to the person at the front desk, "Hello, my name is _____ and I'm here to see [name of person interviewing you]."

- When you enter the interviewer's office, give him or her a friendly smile and shake hands. Do not sit down until you are asked.

- Sit up straight and look at the interviewer when listening and speaking.

- Answer all questions as fully and truthfully as you can, but try to be brief. Speak clearly. Although you may be willing to do anything, there is no job called "anything." Be clear that you are willing to learn all the skills required for the job.

- If the interviewer asks a question you don't understand, say, "I'm sorry, could you repeat that please. I don't quite understand."

- Don't try to be funny, or swear, or use slang. Never talk badly about anyone, especially former employers. Be sure to just answer the questions you are asked, "no storytelling."

- You can ask about wages, hours, or benefits after the job has been offered to you, not before. Chances are the interviewer will tell you about them anyway.

- When the interviewer lets you know the interview is over, ask if you can leave a copy of your resumé, thank him or her, and then leave promptly. On the way out, thank the person at the front desk.

✓

Worksheet 5.10A *continued*

Interviews can seem pretty scary, and most people hate going to them. However, the more interviews you go to, the better you will get at interviewing. Read this section, practice, and you'll end up almost enjoying interviews.

Before you go for an interview, find out a little about the job you are applying for. Practice your answers. If you have any trouble, try *writing* your answers first. Then try to say them aloud. Don't memorize; just try to say what you have written in your own way.

Questions Interviewers May Ask

1. Tell me about yourself.
2. Have you had any experience in this type of work?
3. What are your strengths and weaknesses?
4. What would you like to be doing five years from now?
5. What are your hobbies?
6. What subjects most interested you at school?
7. Do you work well on your own?
8. Do you mind working overtime or on weekends?
9. What do you know about our company?

Questions Interviewers May Not Ask

The Ontario Human Rights Code states that every person has a right to freedom from discrimination on the grounds of:

- race
- ethnicity
- creed
- color
- nationality/citizenship
- ancestry
- place of origin
- sex
- sexual orientation
- marital status/family status
- handicap
- record of offences
- age (18–65 years in employment).

It is normally unacceptable to ask questions dealing with the above matters.

Things to Bring

- a pen (one that works)
- any papers or documents you might need, such as your Social Insurance card, driver's permit, or school reports
- two copies of your resumé – one for the interviewer and one for yourself
- a smile and a positive attitude.

130   © Vicki Lundine and Catherine Smith 2006

WORKSHEET 5.10B: JOB INTERVIEW

You: Hello, my name is _____.

Mr. Smith: Hello _____. Do come in and sit down. How are you today?

You:

Mr. Smith: What job were you interested in?

You:

Mr. Smith: What type of work do you think is involved with this job?

You:

Mr. Smith: Have you done this kind of work before?

You:

Mr. Smith: What are your strengths?

You:

Mr. Smith: What do you consider to be your weaknesses?

You:

Mr. Smith: Tell me about any work you have done before.

You:

Mr. Smith: Would you describe yourself as a hard worker?

You:

Mr. Smith: Do you like working with other people?

You:

Mr. Smith: What days and hours would you be able to work?

You:

Mr. Smith: Do you have any questions?

You:

Mr. Smith: Well, thank you. It was nice meeting you. I will be in touch some time this week.

You:

WORKSHEET 5.10C: PRACTICE INTERVIEW EVALUATION

Date:_____   Name:_____

Communication	☺ Performs well	😐 Satisfactory	☹ Needs improvement
Introduces self with: First name Last name			
Makes eye contact with interviewer			
Offers handshake			
Handshake has firm grip			
Offers resumé			
Answers questions: What type of work do you think is involved with this job? Have you done this kind of work before? What are your strengths?			
Responds appropriately when asked "Do you have any questions?"			
Says "Thank you for the interview"			
Says "Goodbye"			
Offers handshake			

Chapter Six

Job Preparation

Job preparation involves preparing someone to enter the workforce. It fosters the development of positive attitudes and behaviors that will enable that person to be successful when being employed for the first time.

Topics in this chapter examine important work behaviors such as attendance, punctuality, honesty, and communication. A student's attitudes, behaviors and choices in the work experience will provide a basis for future success in the workforce.

Topic 6.1: What's expected on the job

Objective: Students will examine work behaviors that are both acceptable and unacceptable.

Procedure:
1. The teacher explains "What's Expected on the Job" (Activity 6.1A).

2. Through role-play, teacher and students can demonstrate why some behaviors are acceptable while others might be considered unacceptable.

ACTIVITY 6.1A: WHAT'S EXPECTED ON THE JOB

Employers need a person who can demonstrate:

1. Positive attitude

    - be honest
    - look good
    - feel good about yourself
    - work without being told
    - set goals.

2. Thinking skills

    - try new ways of doing things
    - fix problems when they are small
    - think about all parts of a job
    - seek help when the need arises.

3. Responsibility

    - follow instructions
    - be calm
    - check your work
    - be patient
    - be on time
    - follow work rules
    - try to learn more about the job
    - work well by yourself
    - have a positive attitude towards change
    - be proud of your work
    - work neatly
    - keep busy
    - look after equipment (tools)
    - stay on the job
    - try to do the job better each time
    - be ready for work.

4. Health and safety awareness

    - get enough sleep
    - use common sense
    - be physically fit
    - follow safety rules.

Employers need a person who can:

1. Work with others

    - listen to your supervisor/boss
    - be friendly
    - collaborate and work with other people
    - respect other people's belongings
    - respect other people's rights
    - be happy about your job
    - respect privacy.

2. Communicate (talking and listening)

    - ask questions
    - ask for help when you need it
    - phone the office when you are sick
    - speak clearly
    - make eye contact
    - listen actively
    - demonstrate respect
    - be aware of your tone of voice and body language.

Topic 6.2: Positive work behaviors

Objective: Students will become familiar with the vocabulary associated with positive work behaviors.

Procedure: 1. Distribute Worksheet 6.2A and discuss the meaning of each word or phrase.

2. Have students write or verbalize an example of each work behavior listed in Worksheet 6.2A.

WORKSHEET 6.2A: VOCABULARY – POSITIVE WORK BEHAVIORS

As a student, give examples of the work behaviors you already demonstrate:

1. punctual
2. co-operative
3. responsible
4. constructive criticism
5. dependable
6. conscientious
7. industrious
8. able to communicate
9. quality conscious
10. considerate
11. reliable
12. creative
13. respectful
14. organized

Topic 6.3: Attendance rules

Objective: Students will learn the importance of maintaining a habit of good attendance.

Procedure: 1. Discuss with the class the attendance rules described in Activity 6.3A.

2. Distribute Worksheet 6.3B and have students complete this checklist. You may want to lead a class discussion that examines the most common reasons given for missing school or work.

ACTIVITY 6.3A: READ ALL ABOUT IT! ATTENDANCE RULES

An employer depends on employees showing up for work.

If an employee doesn't make it to work, everyone else must work harder in order that all the work gets done.

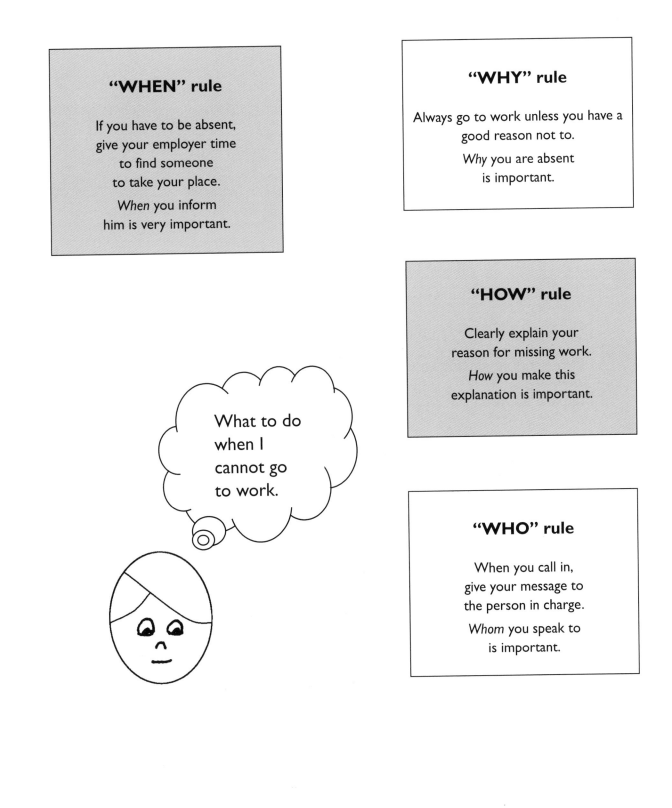

"WHEN" rule

If you have to be absent, give your employer time to find someone to take your place.

When you inform him is very important.

"WHY" rule

Always go to work unless you have a good reason not to.

Why you are absent is important.

"HOW" rule

Clearly explain your reason for missing work.

How you make this explanation is important.

"WHO" rule

When you call in, give your message to the person in charge.

Whom you speak to is important.

What to do when I cannot go to work.

✔

WORKSHEET 6.3B: ABSENTEEISM

I miss work/school because:

☐ I get sick a lot.

☐ I don't like the job.

☐ I'm bored on the job.

☐ I'm not good at the job.

☐ The boss doesn't like me.

☐ I have homework.

☐ I have home problems.

☐ I don't like my boss at work/school.

☐ I have other things to do.

☐ I don't like the people at work/school.

☐ I have trouble getting up in the morning.

☐ I have trouble getting to the job site.

☐ My parents need me to do other things.

☐ I want to go out with my friends who are not working.

☐ I have to babysit.

☐ I'm playing a sport.

☐ I really don't have a reason to be absent.

☐ Other. *Explain your reason:* _____

_____

_____

ABSENTEEISM

Being late or absent could cause many problems for yourself and your employer. Early notification of your absence is helpful.

Topic 6.4: Accepting criticism and praise

Objective: Students will recognize different ways of accepting criticism or praise.

Procedure: 1.   The teacher leads a class discussion about the difference between constructive criticism and negative criticism. Problem-solving cards help visually demonstrate and reinforce the consequences criticism can have on a person and those who hear it. Remind students about the Personal Peak Zones and how words spoken out loud enter into the Personal White Zone of anyone who hears them. A lot of people can be affected by what they hear and how they hear it. This is a good time to reinforce tone of voice and body language as well as the words spoken. Provide an example and then create other examples with the class. Use the thumbs-up or thumbs-down technique to reinforce the effects of each type of criticism.

Example
George arrives at school with a new jacket:

Positive	Effect
Hey, George, nice jacket!	Makes George feel good.
Wow, George, I wish I had your jacket!	This sends a positive message to everyone who hears it. People can be happy for George.

Negative	Effect
Hey George, where did you get that jacket? It's weird! (or teen lingo of the day)	George feels left out, embarrassed, sad, or angry.
Yuuuuk, George. How can you wear that to school?	Not only George feels bad but others may also feel embarrassed for him.

2.   When students have brainstormed a series of positive and negative criticisms, divide the class into small groups. Have them role-play a negative criticism and then follow it with a positive criticism. Discuss how they feel. Reinforce the idea that being able to accept positive criticisms can help them in the workplace as well as in social settings. Students should be aware that it is important to be able to respond to negative criticism as well. This is also a skill that can be discussed and practiced.

3.   When students are out on a work placement, it will be important to debrief with them after each session. If the student is being accompanied by an adult, insure that the adult is tuned in to how the student is responding to any criticisms that he or she may experience. Some students are comfortable sharing this with the class when they meet. These experiences provide real-life encounters that can then be discussed and role-played to help students learn the responses they may need to implement at a future time.

WORKSHEET 6.4A: ACCEPTING CRITICISM AND PRAISE

1. Susan makes out customer receipts in a photography shop. Her supervisor tells her to write more clearly. How should Susan react?

2. Kurt pumps gas at a gas station. He notices a customer's tires are low. He informs the customer. The customer is pleased with Kurt's service and tells the station manager. The manager speaks to Kurt. How should Kurt react?

3. James types in an office. His boss asks him to make fewer errors and to be more careful. How should James handle this advice?

4. Diana works at a dress shop. The manager tells her she would like her to look neater and dress more appropriately. What can Diana do?

5. Doreen works in a bakery. Mrs. Jones comes in to buy some buns and forgets to take her change. Doreen notices the money after Mrs. Jones has left and immediately gives the money to her supervisor. Her supervisor is delighted with Doreen's honesty and tells her. How does Doreen feel?

6. Paula, an assistant in a kindergarten, works with a teacher whom she does not like. The teacher suggests that Paula should be clearer when giving instructions to the children. What should Paula's response be?

7. Pete works as a night janitor. His boss tells him to take more care with his work and to work faster. What can Pete say?

8. Larry is a waiter in a restaurant. The owner mentions that some of the dishes have not been clean and asks Larry to be more careful when setting the tables. What is a good response Larry can give?

Topic 6.5: Signs in the workplace

Objective: Students will review the meaning of various signs in the workplace.

Procedure: 1.   Divide students into pairs and ask each pair to make a particular sign to display in the classroom. Students will need colored paper and/or felt pens.

2.   Students display their signs in the classroom.

3.   When students are going out on a work experience, have them make a list of the signs on the job site and what they mean. They can then report back to the other students in the class.

Note: Students should be encouraged to create signs that inform, command, or warn people. Suggestions to students could include:

RESTRICTED AREA

AUTHORIZED PERSONNEL ONLY

HANDICAPPED PARKING ONLY

EXIT

HELP WANTED

EMPLOYEES ONLY

SMOKING PROHIBITED

HIGH VOLTAGE

FLAMMABLE

EXPLOSIVES

FIRE EXTINGUISHER

Topic 6.6: Confidentiality

Objective: Students will discuss and role-play in order to understand the importance of confidentiality.

Procedure:
1. Discuss what the word "confidentiality" means.

2. Read and discuss the following situations. Why do they require confidentiality?

   - **Hair salon**: Clients really do tell their hairdresser everything. The information that is shared at the hairdresser's should not be repeated. One of the clients may be telling the hairdresser about a surprise birthday party she is planning for her best friend. A woman you know gets her hair dyed and everyone you know always wonders if her hair color is natural. It is something she does not tell people.

   - **Travel agency**: Only the person who is actually purchasing a service from the agency receives any information from the travel agent. Suppose Rob buys two plane tickets. He may be planning a surprise for his wife and he does not want her to find out. They may be planning to be away from home for some time. Their house might be empty. If the wrong people discovered that the house were empty, they might plan to break into the house.

   - **Restaurant**: People often meet in a restaurant to discuss private and confidential matters. Waitresses, waiters and bus boys are expected to keep private information about the people who come to the restaurant. This means they cannot tell others who are in the restaurant whom they are with, what they have to eat or drink, or how much they spend. If the information is shared, it could prove harmful to the restaurant owner because people may stop coming to the restaurant. Anyone found talking about those who eat at the restaurant could be fired.

3. Generate a list of places and situations in which students would be expected to observe confidentiality.

4. Have students role-play different scenarios. Teach them how body language as well as spoken language can give an impression of respect and confidentiality.

Chapter Seven

Career Portfolios: A Demonstration of Skills, Attitudes and Abilities

A number of educators have developed or recognized the need for developing a method that enables students to create career portfolios as they prepare to leave the school system. This is a relatively new concept; therefore, more detail will be provided for those teaching this section of the course.

The career portfolio process confirms that students leaving the school system can demonstrate the values of a well-rounded individual. Completing the portfolio involves a three-year process before the student graduates. In this manual the authors refer to the process they have helped implement in British Columbia, Canada. In this process students are supported as they learn how to recognize and sort relevant experiences under six headings or organizers within their career portfolios. These include: "Art and design"; "Community involvement and responsibility"; "Education and career planning"; "Employability skills"; "Information technology"; and "Personal health." Other schemes may use different headings, but their overall aim will be very similar. The process encourages students to:

- explore their strengths, interests, values and capabilities in order to help them recognize themselves as unique individuals

- collect pertinent data that reflects their involvement and skills in the six areas covered in the portfolio

- organize relevant data into a format whereby they can demonstrate their personal strengths and values

- develop realistic personal and career goals based on the information they gather.

Many programs that focus on teaching career and personal planning skills to students with ASD and other developmental disabilities have been fostering this process for a number of years. The following lessons, which have been developed over the past 15 years, are a natural extension of the work that the authors have been creating for students with ASD and other developmental disabilities.

Although this chapter appears near the end of the book, it is recommended that the concepts in this unit be introduced to students early in the course. The concepts presented elsewhere in the manual can be related to different aspects of the six themes that make up the career portfolio. Teachers can help students recognize how the topics they are learning relate to the six themes. For example:

- **Community involvement and responsibility**: Chapter Two, "Self-awareness," helps students recognize their roles in their community – the groups and activities they attend, and the volunteer work they may perform.

- **Education and career planning**: Chapter Five, "Career Awareness," and Chapter Six, "Job Preparation," help students recognize and focus on the aspects that will prepare them for a career.

- **Personal health**: Chapter Three, "Life Skills," provides opportunities for students to discuss and demonstrate good grooming, proper nutrition and participation in community sports and activities to promote a healthy lifestyle.

By the time students are ready to leave the school system, they should be prepared to present their portfolios to a prospective employer. As already mentioned, creating career portfolios is a process which students can begin up to three years before they leave school. The skills which students develop by participating in this process can support them well into adulthood. Learning job skills, role-playing, and participating in work experience programs are critical elements of a career preparation course. Students must also be capable of producing evidence to demonstrate their ability to participate in the workforce. Even when teachers and parents are confident that students have achieved successful learning outcomes on the course, they cannot assume that students will be able to recall or recognize the value of their experiences. Creating a career portfolio provides the concrete evidence that allows them to track the skills they are acquiring.

Students must be taught how to recognize relevant portfolio material and maintain up-to-date information that clearly demonstrates their achievements. Those who learn to define the essential elements that promote their qualifications for a job will approach the workforce with a valuable passport. Having a well organized portfolio that contains pertinent information helps a student to present evidence of his or her skills in an interview with confidence. Portfolios remain a testament to a student's achievements.

What is a portfolio?

It is a compilation of relevant information about a student's skills, abilities, interests and values that can be presented either in an electronic or a physical format. The career portfolio covers the six themes stated above. Students should be able to demonstrate knowledge and experience in all of the six theme areas. The activities included in this chapter:

- introduce and explain the terminology

- provide students with opportunities to explore how these themes reflect their communities as they list leisure and career opportunities that are available to them

- help students recognize their personal involvement in their community

- clarify the skills, knowledge and values students have acquired in these areas

- provide worksheets for students to record relevant information that demonstrates their capabilities and interests

- promote practice in recording the evidence that supports the information students provide.

The authors strongly advise that teachers and parents supporting students through this process establish a consistent review schedule. This will allow students to revise the information in their career portfolios to insure that their information remains current and relevant.

What does the portfolio contain?

The portfolio contains information that reflects the values that employers appreciate. These values include the ability to:

- listen

- learn

- communicate effectively

- be responsible

- be reliable

- set and achieve goals

- work with others

- problem-solve independently and with others

- demonstrate respect by dressing and grooming appropriately
- take initiative.

What exactly does that look like?

The portfolio is a portable vehicle that is easily accessible, organized, current, pertinent and succinct. It contains evidence of the student's skills, values and abilities as experienced at school, in the community and in work placements. Evidence may include:

- letters of reference
- samples of work and participation in community functions
- evaluation forms
- certificates
- photos
- videos
- PowerPoint presentations.

The portfolio may take the form of an album, a video, a folder, a journal, a collage, a written summary, PowerPoint or live presentation, or a box. The method for presenting a student's information will depend on the place where the student is presenting the information as well as the person or persons to whom it is being presented. It is recommended that whenever possible the information be transcribed onto a CD. A CD is portable, provides a back-up of the evidence, and can be updated with little effort.

For students who may have communication and/or cognitive challenges, using digital photos to demonstrate their achievements and experiences can act as triggers to help them represent themselves with greater confidence. For example, consider an individual who becomes over-anxious when asked to interact spontaneously. The individual's stress can be alleviated significantly when he is able to present a portfolio that includes photos of him:

- accepting an award for participating in a Special Olympics event
- greeting people at the church entrance
- assisting a peer in a swim program
- playing the piano for a group of seniors
- harvesting pumpkins on a farm
- preparing food in a restaurant
- showing a customer where to find items in a store

- loading scraps in a wastebin on a construction site

- skiing with a group of friends

- being awarded a badge of merit in a youth group

- shaking hands with employers who have mentored the student in work experience placements

- working at a computer.

The photos enable the employer and student to engage in a meaningful conversation about the student's talents and interests. This can significantly enhance an employer's appreciation of the student's capabilities.

Would all portfolios include photos?

Not necessarily. The portfolios that are presented can be as diverse as the individuals in the course. A student may produce letters of recommendation, provide written evidence of collaboration on exhibits or of assisting others, and show samples of his or her work. However, a picture is worth a thousand words. If pictures help promote aspects of the student that might otherwise be missed, then including photos is definitely worth considering.

Who is responsible for helping a student acquire evidence for the portfolio?

A student with ASD or other developmental disabilities often has a team of people supporting him or her. Each person on a team can participate in helping a student recognize the experiences he or she has had, and how these reflect skills and abilities valued by the community and employers. Parents and teachers must maintain a collaborative partnership in defining the roles each member of the student's team will play in supporting a student as he or she develops a portfolio. They can do this by helping to insure the student understands and demonstrates the ability to:

- recognize relevant experiences that can be included in a portfolio

- access evidence to reflect the success of the experiences

- organize the evidence

- record evidence

- store the evidence in a safe and accessible location

- maintain an up-to-date portfolio.

Parents also play a vital role in organizing support personnel who may be supporting their child's involvement in sports or community activities. Support personnel may be asked to record their son or daughter:

- interacting with others
- assisting others
- training
- learning new skills
- accomplishing tasks
- participating in group activities
- competing
- receiving recognition for his or her participation in an event.

Support personnel can be critical liaisons in helping to collect pertinent information that reflects the student's capabilities, as they may be the only representative of the team attending an event or activity with the student.

A student's peer group is another important resource in helping a student recognize some of the gifts and talents he or she brings to the school. Peers who have grown up with students with ASD and other developmental disabilities often provide unique perspectives about the student because they have been in daily contact with him or her on a different level. Peers can be resourceful supports in helping a student:

- recognize unique skills and talents
- collect evidence
- sort evidence
- organize evidence
- present portfolios.

Never underestimate the creative power of peers who have been an integral part of a student's life. They are invaluable.

Where is original documentation stored?

Ultimately, when students leave school, they will continue to upgrade their portfolios. It is important that students appreciate that the evidence they collect needs to be stored in a safe place where they have easy access to it. While at school, the teacher may require access to the information in order to be able to help students learn how to organize it. Photocopies of original documents or photos of awards or medals should be sent to the school. Originals should remain with the student and his family. If awards or other mementos are being shown in a presentation, the student should take them home after the presentation.

How can the team help students recognize the skills they are acquiring so students learn to reference them?

Most teams are very conscientious about recognizing and recording skills which students are learning and applying. Teachers, parents, caregivers and para-professionals must also recognize the importance of insuring that students are aware of the skills they are learning and how important those skills are for their future success. Students often do not recognize that the skills they are learning in one environment can easily transfer to other environments and people. In fact, according to many employment counselors, typical students are not always aware of this. In order to help students transfer and generalize the skills they are acquiring, it is critical that students be reminded of how portable their skills are.

Example 1: A student signed up to open the school concession stand, work as a cashier and deliver the cash to the office at the end of lunch. She successfully and conscientiously performed the job for the term she was assigned the responsibility. This student should understand that, when she is applying for a job, she can report that she is honest, responsible and reliable. In addition to being able to state these qualities, she can ask the supervisor in charge of the canteen for a letter of reference that reflects these qualities.

Example 2: A student is working in the school canteen and has learned to use the cash register. The supervisor who is teaching him these skills should point out that these are the same skills he would use if he were to work as a cashier at the corner store, in a shop in the mall or at a gas station. Once again, do not assume that the student will see the connection between the skills he is using in the canteen and a job in another location.

Example 3: A student learns to wave and smile when leaving the job site. She is demonstrating good interpersonal skills that demonstrate job satisfaction, appreciation and a willingness to be a part of that community. People like to work with people who appreciate the roles they have. Students need to be aware that these are valuable skills which they can report in a resumé.

The career portfolio is designed to help all students access employment in their community and to pursue healthy lifestyles. It also provides an avenue that celebrates a student's gifts and talents. It is a process that truly helps people to look beyond the labels.

Topic 7.1: Understanding the terms

Objective: Students will become familiar with the terms associated with the themes in the personal portfolios.

Procedure: Provide each student with the list of themes they will use to organize their portfolios. Include a graphic that illustrates the theme for those students who require picture support. The themes include: "Art and design"; "Community involvement and responsibility"; "Education and career planning"; "Employability skills"; "Information technology"; and "Personal health."

Provide each student with a Portfolio Theme Box Chart for Activity 1 and Individual Portfolio Charts for Activity 2. The teacher can create a large Portfolio Theme Box Chart on the board or use chart paper which has a theme written on each page for Activity 1. Use chart paper for Activity 2. Insure students have materials to create collages or posters for Activity 3.

ACTIVITY 1: GROUP ACTIVITY

- Write each theme heading on the board, an overhead, or chart paper.

- Provide students with a copy of the Portfolio Theme Chart (Worksheet 7.1A).

- Help students understand the terms by providing them with the examples below:

  1. *Art and design*: paint, listen to music, gardening, collections

  2. *Community involvement and responsibility*: attend church clubs, participate in Special Olympics, therapeutic riding

  3. *Education and career planning*: high school, career training and personal planning course; home economics course

  4. *Employability skills*: babysitter, church greeter, dish washer

  5. *Information technology*: use a Voice Output Communication Aid (VOCA), create PowerPoint presentations

  6. *Personal health*: good nutrition, exercise, swim, ski, ride bike.

- Have students transcribe these examples onto their Portfolio Theme Charts.

- Ask students to consider experiences they have had and activities they are presently involved in, or have participated in, and to think about which box they can put them in.

- Transcribe them onto the chart paper and have students record the answers on their sheets.

- Help students to categorize these activities under the correct theme headings.

- Insure all members of the class can understand.

ACTIVITY 2

Give each student a copy of the Individual Portfolio Theme Charts (Worksheet 7.1B).

- Have students work in pairs or in small groups.

- Ask students to list all the activities or experiences they can remember having had.

- Then ask them to categorize these under the proper theme headings.

- Mount six pieces of chart paper. Label each with one of the six theme headings.

- Ask students to share their answers and transcribe the answers onto the corresponding chart paper.

- Record the answers so each student has a copy for future use.

ACTIVITY 3

Have students create posters or collages that include activities that reflect the meaning of each heading.

- Students may be assigned a theme to illustrate.

- Students may create a collage or poster that reflects all of the portfolio themes.

- Encourage students to share their collages or posters.

HOME AND SCHOOL PARTNERSHIP

Have students take their assignments home to share with their family who will then become familiar with the themes their child is exploring.

WORKSHEET 7.1A: PORTFOLIO THEME CHART

ART AND DESIGN	COMMUNITY INVOLVEMENT AND RESPONSIBILITY
EDUCATION AND CAREER PLANNING	EMPLOYABILITY SKILLS
INFORMATION TECHNOLOGY	PERSONAL HEALTH

WORKSHEET 7.1B: INDIVIDUAL PORTFOLIO THEME CHARTS

ART AND DESIGN

COMMUNITY INVOLVEMENT AND RESPONSIBILITY

✓

EDUCATION AND CAREER PLANNING

EMPLOYABILITY SKILLS

✓

INFORMATION TECHNOLOGY

PERSONAL HEALTH

Topic 7.2: Making connections

Objective: Students will begin to recognize how their participation and responsibilities at home, at school and in the community can be applied to a career portfolio. Students will also become familiar with people and places in the community that reflect the careers within each theme.

Procedure: Provide different colored markers for students to record answers. Label six pieces of chart paper with one of the themes: "Art and design"; "Community involvement and responsibility"; "Education and career planning"; "Employability skills"; "Information technology"; and "Personal health."

Divide each chart into six sections. Label the sections as follows:

1.   Courses I take at school

2.   School activities

3.   Community activities

4.   Careers

5.   People we know in these careers

6.   Things I do.

Explain to students that they will record answers to the statements listed under the headings. They will have to think about how the statement relates their experiences in that particular area being examined. Students can be given a set time and then be directed to the next chart.

Example:
Technology skills

1.   *Courses I take at school:* computer classes, video editing, use the software package Co-Writer for journal in English class, sew with computerized sewing machine.

2.   *School activities:* submit reports for newspaper, take digital photos of class events, import pictures for my journal, run the DVD machine in life skills class, set up the CD player for teacher, use the microwave oven to heat lunches.

3. *Community activities*: write letters on computer for seniors, participate in local drama using a VOCA, take digital photos of group outings.

4. *Careers*: sales, programmer, cashier, illustrator, technician, teacher, machinist, seamstress, cook.

5. *Things I do with technology*: E-mail my friends, send text messages, use the DVD player, download music, heat my dinner, play video games, find information on the web.

ACTIVITY

Divide students into groups. Provide each group with a colored pen. Assign each group to one of the six charts. As a group, ask the students to write/illustrate their answers to the five sections on their chart. Tell them, if they get stuck, to go on to the next section in the chart and come back if there is time at the end. Determine how much time each group should spend on their chart. When time is up ask students to move to the next chart.

Provide students with an opportunity to read and add to each theme. Share the answers that students generate.

Record all answers for future reference. Provide each student with his or her own copy. For students who require illustrations or photos, these can be prepared ahead of time and placed near the charts so that students can choose and paste them on the chart, or these can be added at a later date. Charts that are completed in class can be photographed digitally and then pasted onto a document for distribution to students. The information can also be e-mailed to those students and parents who have computers at home.

HOME AND SCHOOL PARTNERSHIP

Parents can support students in recognizing further connections to the different themes by discussing the activities, opportunities, people and places that reflect their personal experiences. For example, Mom is a teacher, Dad is a welder, sister is a dancer, one neighbor is an artist, and another neighbor is a ski-lift operator. Digital photos can be used to illustrate the information and make it more meaningful for those students who require further visual support.

WORKSHEET 7.2A: MAKING PERSONAL CONNECTIONS

Theme
Courses I take at school that reflect this theme:
School activities that reflect this theme:
Community activities that reflect this theme:
Careers that reflect this theme:
People we know in these careers:
Things I do that reflect this theme:

Topic 7.3: Sorting evidence

Objective: Students will begin to recognize what evidence to access to support experiences they wish to use in a career portfolio.

Procedure: Provide each student with a blank copy of Worksheet 7.3A, "Theme Evidence," and Worksheet 7.3B, "Portfolio Theme Chart."

ACTIVITY 1

Ask students to cut and paste the appropriate strip from Worksheet 7.3A into the appropriate boxes on Worksheet 7.3B.

HOME AND SCHOOL PARTNERSHIP

Ask students to take the assignment home and share it with parents. Parents can begin to talk to students about the evidence they may have at home, or can obtain, which reflects experiences their son or daughter has had.

Participation ribbon from a community recreation activity	Thank-you note for helping a neighbour	Resumé
Video created in school	Volunteer recognition award	Video taken at a cultural event
Evidence of participation in a martial arts program	Picture of a meal prepared in the cafeteria program	Superhost certicate
Newspaper article of participation in a sporting event	FoodSafe certificate	Work experience log sheet
Picture of you with your Special Olympics team-mates	Work experience evaluation	Letter from teacher on your assistance with a project
Letter of reference	Report on graduation transition plan	Picture of participation in Special Olympic event
Self-evaluation of your work experience	Your own example	Your own example

WORKSHEET 7.3B: PORTFOLIO THEME CHART

ART AND DESIGN	COMMUNITY INVOLVEMENT AND RESPONSIBILITY
EDUCATION AND CAREER PLANNING	EMPLOYABILITY SKILLS
INFORMATION TECHNOLOGY	PERSONAL HEALTH

Topic 7.4: Sorting information for career portfolios

Objective: Students will begin to select information and sort personal information under the appropriate theme.

Procedure: Insure students have the information collected from Worksheets 7.1B and 7.2A. Provide students with Worksheet 7.4A, "Personal Career Portfolio Chart." Highlighters would be beneficial.

- Remind students that as they gather information about the different themes, they can begin to recognize how they spend their time, what they like to do, how well they do in certain areas.

- Remind students that each person is an individual and so not all the information will apply to each one of them.

- Encourage them to consider more activities they may do with family and friends that can go into the "Experience" column.

- Students may work independently or in small groups.

- Complete the "Experience" column only.

HOME AND SCHOOL PARTNERSHIP

Parents can support their son or daughter in reminding them of experiences that might apply to their Personal Career Portfolio Chart. They may have photographs or certificates that reflect their son or daughter's experiences which they can help record on the Personal Career Portfolio Chart.

WORKSHEET 7.4A: PERSONAL CAREER PORTFOLIO CHART

Art and design		
Experience	**Evidence**	**Recording evidence**

Community involvement and responsibility		
Experience	**Evidence**	**Recording evidence**

Education and career planning		
Experience	**Evidence**	**Recording evidence**

✓

Employability skills		
Experience	**Evidence**	**Recording evidence**

Information technology		
Experience	**Evidence**	**Recording evidence**

Personal health		
Experience	**Evidence**	**Recording evidence**

Topic 7.5: Collecting evidence

Objective: Students will collect evidence to demonstrate the information recorded on their Personal Career Portfolio Charts.

Procedure: Insure each student has a copy of their Personal Career Portfolio Chart on which they have completed the "Experience" column.

ACTIVITY

- Beside each response the students have recorded in the "Experience" column ask them to draw a line through any information that is not currently relevant.

- Once the students complete this, ask them to write down what evidence they have to validate the experiences they have recorded.

- Complete "Experience" and "Evidence" columns only.

For example:

Community responsibility and involvement		
Experience	**Evidence**	**Recording evidence**
Give piano concerts for seniors	senior's calendar	
Greet people at church	letter from minister	
Weed community garden	photograph	
~~Sell cupcakes for Grade 3 class~~		
Walk neighbor's dog	letter from neighbor	

Topic 7.6: Recording the evidence

Objective: Students will develop a system to provide manageable evidence of the information that has been collected for their career portfolios.

Procedure:

- Insure each student has a copy of their Personal Career Portfolio Chart on which they have completed the "Experience" and "Evidence" columns.

- Encourage students to consider how they can provide manageable evidence for the information they have provided on their Personal Career Portfolio Charts.

- Inform students that they will now complete the column "Recording evidence" on their Personal Career Portfolio Charts.

ACTIVITY

Discuss the importance of validating the statements that students have recorded in the "Experience" columns. Then have them reflect on the feasibility of carting boxes of evidence around when going out for interviews. How practical would that be? Have them think about ways they can present their evidence in a clear and concise manner. In the "Recording evidence" column, have students consider the format they will use to demonstrate the skill they have cited. *For example*: Gold medal winner in Special Olympics competition – the student can provide a photo of himself on the podium receiving the medal, he could obtain a letter from his coach, he could use the coach as a reference, or he could photocopy a newspaper article. Have students complete the "Recording evidence" columns of their Personal Career Portfolio Chart.

HOME AND SCHOOL PARTNERSHIP

Have students take their charts home and determine if the format they have chosen to present evidence is possible. It will not be necessary to actually complete the recording yet, as students will still have to reflect on their information and prioritize it.

Topic 7.7: Reflecting and selecting critical evidence

Objective: Students will be able to select the most relevant information recorded on their Personal Career Portfolio Charts to be included in their career portfolios.

Procedure: Insure each student has a completed Personal Career Portfolio Chart and a highlighter or colored pen.

ACTIVITY

Ask students to think about what they consider to be the three most important facts that they have recorded on each theme in their charts. Inform them that they must be very selective about the information they are going to include in their career portfolios. The career portfolio has to reflect who they are, what values they hold, and what they are capable of doing, by highlighting the most important information they have collected. What they choose will have to relay their message clearly in a limited amount of time. Once they have completed this activity, students can begin to think about the method they plan to use to present their information.

HOME AND SCHOOL PARTNERSHIP

Parents can support the choices that their son or daughter has made in this process and insure that the evidence can be provided in the format that has been recorded.

Topic 7.8: Choosing a presentation format

Objective: Students will decide on a format to present the information that they have recorded in their Personal Career Portfolio Charts.

Procedure: Access pictures of, or samples of, a variety of methods students can choose to create a career portfolio. A career portfolio can be presented electronically using a PowerPoint presentation that includes photos, short video clips and/or scanned documents. It can also be presented in hard copy as a photo journal, an album, a journal, a file, a video, a presentation, or a demonstration. The way a student presents his or her career portfolio can be tailored to the person or panel with whom he or she will be sharing the information.

ACTIVITY

Students will choose a format and organize the details for collating the information they have gathered during the process. They will complete the career portfolio and schedule dates to review the information regularly with the teacher. It is recommended that students and teacher review the career portfolios every three months, or whenever the student has more current information to add to or replace in the career portfolio. When a student's career portfolio is completed and/or revised, each student will practice presenting the information.

- Begin by asking students to choose a person with whom they are comfortable sharing the information.

- Have students practice their presentations.

- Encourage the students to then present to a small group of peers.

- If possible, enlist colleagues who would be willing to participate in the process of getting students comfortable presenting their portfolios.

- Remind students they can practice with parents and relatives and in front of the mirror at home as well.

HOME AND SCHOOL PARTNERSHIP

Parents can support their children to become comfortable presenting the information from the career portfolio by listening to them. Parents can be supportive by allowing their child to make mistakes as he or she gets familiar with the information and the process. It can be a pretty intimidating task, but practice makes perfect. As each student becomes comfortable with the material and has opportunities to try it out with supportive family and friends, his or her confidence and delivery will improve.

Chapter Eight

Connections

All students, including those with special needs, have the right to engage in a process that provides them with opportunities to participate in the world of work. This manual addresses a wide range of topics designed to help students enhance life skills, decision-making, goal-setting, career awareness and job preparation. The curriculum defines skills and abilities which students require in order to be successful in the workplace. When a team also combines teaching these skills with access to meaningful work experiences, students acquire greater opportunities to explore their strengths, talents, interests and challenges. Students gain insights into jobs they may wish to pursue, as well as jobs they may choose to avoid. They can begin to determine if their talents may lead to a career or be best nurtured as an avocation. Combining the curriculum with real work opportunities helps students to recognize the value of learning and applying skills that can help to increase their prospects for employment.

The home–school–community partnership helps to take the "dis-" out of disabilities. Trainers, citizens and employers begin to look beyond labels and see past first impressions. The atmosphere of collaboration and cooperation created by these partnerships has the potential to synergize everyone who becomes involved in the process.

The students begin to see themselves as integral, contributing members of a working community. Today, a number of graduates from this program not only hold paying positions, they volunteer their time playing piano for elderly citizens, caring for animals at the local shelter, spending time interacting with younger children with challenges, and helping raise funds for charity. These young adults recognize and are proud of their contributions. Their participation in the community continues to keep them visible, active and involved.

Peers can become powerful allies for individuals with ASD and other developmental disabilities. Once peers have had some training around a diagnosis and are taught strategies about how to support each other, they prove to be invaluable. They soon recognize the talents, strengths, interests and fears that these students demonstrate. Not only are many peers willing to encourage these students, some have gone on to become teachers, para-professionals, medical specialists and social workers. What begins as a secondary school interest can lead to a career and a lifestyle. The connections that peers make with students who have challenges is of critical importance because they are the ones who are the future caregivers, employers and advocates for many of the students with whom they attend school.

Parents appreciate a structured program that assists their child in becoming a full participant in the community. A career training program provides parents with encouragement and hope. They see their son or daughter getting ready for an interview, organizing a career portfolio, working side-by-side with typical workers in a work setting, accessing transportation and talking about their jobs with peers. Parents watch as their son or daughter experiences the same process as his or her peers and siblings.

School personnel are in a unique position to significantly influence student success. By continuing to teach and train students safe environments where they have opportunities to explore career options, teachers in secondary schools validate all of the time and planning that has preceded this stage in the student's life. It is important to acknowledge the time and dedication of those who supported students throughout their earlier programs as they acquired such fundamental skills as joint attention, waiting, greeting, taking turns, and self-regulation. All of these, and many other basic skills, provide an important foundation for the career training program.

The authors have had a number of heartwarming experiences that truly represent the importance of teaching all aspects of career development. Take, for example, Rob. He had his first interview during the class session and returned before the class ended. One of the students asked if he had been given the job. Rob smiled from ear to ear and confidently announced, "Yes, I did, and it is all because I stood tall, looked Mr. James in the eye, shook his hand and said 'Thank you for seeing me.'" The class soundly congratulated Rob. To insure that this very important skill had become an intrinsic part of the students' repertoire, students were met at the door every session by the teacher to practice the skills involved in greeting and saying goodbye to a prospective employer.

John provided another example. He was learning how to (1) recognize when he had a problem; (2) how to define the problem; and (3) how to develop strategies to cope with the problem using a T chart (see page 94). When he first completed a form on "Being bullied" he commented, "I didn't know that I could do something about it." It isn't that John had not had lectures on bullying, he did not realize at the time that the concepts applied to him. When he became actively involved in filling in his own personal form, he became empowered to address the problem.

Employers provide a reality to the program that enhances everything that is being done by all the other members of the team. They provide opportunities for students to have firsthand experiences in a variety of work placements to see whether or not the student enjoys doing the job. This allows the student to apply the skills in a real job situation.

Employers who were approached to consider taking on a student with autism in the workplace were provided with the necessary information and support to help them get to know the students as individuals. Many reported that they found the students not only learned the jobs they were assigned, but could also be challenged to increase their level of participation and output. Many employers recognized that they could justify giving legitimate jobs to these individuals. It reinforced, for many employers, the point that charity donations do not meet the needs of the students because donations do not provide training opportunities. Some businessmen and -women not only recognized their social responsibilities, they also enlisted the support of others by sharing their experiences in forums such as Rotary Club lunches. In addition, key issues regarding community access, transportation, and effective, efficient and safe working conditions, which affected a number of other individuals in the community, were addressed.

The home–school–community partnerships which have been established by jointly addressing the issues around career options for students with ASD and other developmental disabilities has created an atmosphere of respect and appreciation for the role that each has to play in order to contribute to the success of a community. We often hear that it takes a village to raise a community. However, the authors have learned on more than one occasion that it sometimes takes a child to raise a village.

Appendix

- Work experience course checklist
- Sample task analysis: Record of student performance
- Task analysis: Record of student performance
- Career preparation: Student registration form
- Work-site agreement of confidentiality
- Work experience program: Safety questionnaire
- Work experience program: Student daily log
- First aid record

WORK EXPERIENCE COURSE CHECKLIST

To be filled in by the teacher.

Student name:_____ Date of birth:_____

	N/A (dated)	Introduction (dated)	Has to learn (dated)			Mastered (dated)
			Weak	Moderate	Strong	
SELF-AWARENESS						
a. Self exploration						
b. Life's path						
c. Strengths						
d. Personal and sexual awareness						
e. Appropriate self expression						
LIFE SKILLS						
a. Personal health maintenance						
b. Time management						
c. Money management						
d. Community awareness						
e. Conversation skills						
f. Telephone skills						
DECISION-MAKING AND GOAL-SETTING						
a. Decision-making						
b. Goal-setting						

	N/A (dated)	Introduction (dated)	Has to learn (dated)			Mastered (dated)
			Weak	*Moderate*	*Strong*	
CAREER AWARENESS						
a. Job opportunities in community						
b. Occupational search						
c. Job search						
d. SIN application						
e. General application forms						
f. Support agencies						
g. Resumé						
h. Interview						
JOB PREPARATION						
a. Expectations						
b. Criticism/praise						
c. Signs in workplace						
CAREER PORTFOLIO						
a. Lists personal experiences under designated themes						
b. Selects relevant experiences						
c. Provides evidence of experiences						
d. Creates career portfolio						
e. Maintains up-to-date career portfolio						
f. Presents portfolio information						

✓

Work experience course checklist *continued*

	N/A (dated)	Introduction (dated)	Has to learn (dated)			Mastered (dated)
			Weak	Moderate	Strong	
OTHER						
a.						
b.						
c.						
d.						
e.						
f.						
g.						

Signatures: Student _____

Parent _____

Teacher _____

✔

SAMPLE TASK ANALYSIS: RECORD OF STUDENT PERFORMANCE

Student: Mary Smith   Grade: 12
School: CR Senior Secondary
Supervisor: John Doe
Placement: CR Pet Center

Date	Feb 20	Feb 27	Mar 5	Mar 12	Mar 26
Purse and coat in proper place.	✓	✓	✗	✓	✓
Spot vacuum – front door area, small animals and birds.	✓	✓	✓	✓	✓
Check animals – clean, water and feed if necessary.	✓	✓	✓	✓	✓
Spray reptiles (use warm water).	✓	✓	✓	✓	✓
Wipe down aquariums – fish wall.	✓	✓	✓	✓	✓
Check and remove any dead fish and dispose of them.	✓	✓	✓	✓	✓
Ask about any dusting and sweeping.	✓	✗	✓	✓	✓
Last 15 minutes Mary is free to play with the animals.	✓	✓	✓	✓	✓
Eventually it would be good if Mary was able to stand at the till area and help bag purchases.					✓

TASK ANALYSIS: RECORD OF STUDENT PERFORMANCE

Student: Grade:
School:
Supervisor:
Placement:

Date					

CAREER PREPARATION: STUDENT REGISTRATION FORM

DATE: _____

PERSONAL INFORMATION:

Name: _____ Former last name: _____
     First   Middle   Last

Female _____ Male _____ Date of birth: _____
                                     Month   Day   Year

Address: _____
City: _____ Postal code /ZIP code: _____ Home phone: _____
E-mail: _____ Work phone: _____

CITIZENSHIP: Country of birth or permanent resident _____ Other _____

PREVIOUS EDUCATION:

Do you have a Graduation Diploma? Yes _____ No _____
If no, do you have any course credits? Yes _____ No _____
Last school attended: _____ City: _____
Number of years out of school: _____
I heard about Continuing Education from: Friend/relative ☐ School ☐ Agency ☐
TV ☐ Newspaper ☐ Poster/brochure ☐ Sign ☐ Website ☐ Other _____
My computer skills (circle one):   none   low   some   high
                                         0   1   2   3   4   5

IN CASE OF EMERGENCY CONTACT:

Name: _____ Home phone: _____
Relationship: _____ Work phone: _____
Do you have a Medical Alert condition? _____
Other health concerns staff should be aware of: _____
_____

FOR SPONSORED STUDENTS ONLY:

Information about my current and past activities as a student at Continuing Education
may be made available to the sponsoring agency named on this form.

Yes _____ No _____ Signature: _____

FOR OFFICE USE ONLY:

Method of Payment:
Self Paying: _____ Sponsor: _____
Goal: _____

WORK-SITE AGREEMENT OF CONFIDENTIALITY

To Students and Parents:

It is important that students be aware of the importance of confidentiality of information learned while at a work site.

The **Freedom of Information and Protection of Privacy Act** declares that it is an offense to use or disclose personal information learned at a work site for any reason other than as necessary in the job. Personal information includes: name, address, phone numbers, ethnicity, religion, age, marital status, education, employment, medical or psychiatric history.

It is ethically wrong to disclose other sensitive information learned while at a work site. Information such as details of children at a day care center or client data in a business is to be kept confidential.

Students are asked to sign the following agreement of confidentiality prior to starting work at a work site.

Student name: _____

I hereby agree that I will not, either now or after ceasing my work experience, disclose or otherwise use any personal information or sensitive company information I learned while working at:_____

Date: _____ Signature: _____

**ORIGINAL TO BE RETURNED TO SCHOOL BY STUDENT
AND HELD FOR ONE (1) YEAR.**

✓

WORK EXPERIENCE PROGRAM: SAFETY QUESTIONNAIRE

Student name: _____ Date: _____

Supervisor interviewed: _____ Company: _____

Please ask your supervisor the following safety questions on the first day of your placement. Hand in this questionnaire with your first timesheet when you return to school.

1. What are the dangers of my job?

2. Are there any other hazards (noise, chemical, radiation) that I should know about?

3. Is there any specialized clothing or equipment I need? If so, what is it?

4. Will I require safety training? Yes ☐ No ☐

   If yes, what is it?

5. Are there emergency procedures I need to be trained in (chemical spill, fire, etc.)?

6. Where are the fire extinguishers, first-aid kits and other emergency equipment located?

7. What are my health and safety responsibilities?

8. Whom do I ask if I have a health or safety question?

9. What do I do if I get hurt? Whom should I see if I get hurt?

First aid person's name: _____

I have been interviewed by: _____

Supervisor's signature

✓

WORK EXPERIENCE PROGRAM: STUDENT DAILY LOG

Student's name: _____   Date: _____

School: _____   Company: _____

Briefly describe the work which you participated in or observed each day. Please note your own growth in confidence, abilities, interest, etc., each working day. Be sure to complete the form at the end of every work day.

Days/hours	Various activities carried out each day
Date: Hours worked:	
Date: Hours worked:	
Date: Hours worked:	
Date: Hours worked:	
Date: Hours worked:	

_____   _____
Employer's/supervisor's signature   Student's signature

Please use the reverse side of this form for comments.

FIRST AID RECORD

Date of injury or illness	Time of injury or illness
Name	Time and date reported
Occupation	
Description of injury or report of illness (what happened)	
Nature of injury or illness (signs and symptoms)	
Treatment(s)	
First aid attendant's signature	First aid attendant's name
Patient's signature	
Names of witnesses 1. 2. 3.	
Referral of case and remarks (return to work/medical aid/ambulance)	

Resources

Bibliography

Alberta Learning and Teaching Resources Branch (1995) *Essential and Supportive Skills for Students with Developmental Disabilities.* Edmonton, AB: Learning Resources Centre, Government of Alberta. (www.lrc.learning.gov.ab.ca)

Alberta Learning and Teaching Resources Branch (2003) *Teaching Students with Autism Spectrum Disorders.* Edmonton, AB: Learning Resources Centre, Government of Alberta. (www.lrc.learning.gov.ab.ca)

Attwood, T. (1998) *Asperger's Syndrome: A guide for parents and professionals.* London: Jessica Kingsley Publishers.

Conference Board of Canada (2000) *Employability Skills 2000+.* Ottawa, ON: Conference Board of Canada.

Fownes, L. (2005) *Making the Transfer: Essential skills at work.* Workshop presentation, National Consultation on Career Development (NATCON), Ottawa, ON, 24–26 January.

Gillis, G. (1995) *Career Development Handbook.* Campbell River, BC: Campbell River School District #72.

Grandin, T. (2000) 'My experiences with visual thinking, sensory problems and communication difficulties.' www.autism.org/temple/visual.html

Grandin, T. and Duffy, K. (2004) *Developing Talents: Careers for individuals with Asperger Syndrome and high functioning autism.* Shawnee Mission, KS: Autism Asperger Publishing Company.

Gray, C. A. (1999) *From Both Sides Now: Teaching social understanding with Social Stories and comic strip conversations.* (Available from The Gray Center for Social Learning and Understanding, 2020 Raybrook SE, Suite 101, Grand Rapids, MI, USA. www.thegraycenter.org)

Groden, J., LeVasseur, P., Diller, A. and Cautela, J. (2002) *Coping with Stress through Picture Rehearsal: A how-to manual for working with individuals with autism and developmental disabilities.* Providence, RI: Groden Center.

Hodgdon, L. (1995) *Visual Strategies for Improving Communication: Practical supports for home and school.* Troy, MI: QuirkRoberts Publishing.

Hodgdon, L. (1999) *Solving Behavior Problems in Autism: Improving communication with visual strategies.* Troy, MI: QuirkRoberts Publishing.

Hutchinson, N. L. and Freeman, J. G. (1994) *Pathways (Five-volume career education program).* Scarborough, ON: ITP Nelson, Canada.

Jamieson, M., Paterson, J., Krupa, T., MacEachen, E. and Topping, A. (1993) *Thresholds.* Kingston, ON: Canadian Guidance and Counselling Foundation.

Misener, J. and Butler, S. (2000) *Horizons 2000+ Career Studies.* Toronto, ON: McGraw-Hill Ryerson Ltd.

Misener, J. and Kearns, S. (1993) *Expanding your Horizons.* Toronto, ON: McGraw-Hill Ryerson Ltd.

Moedt, M. (not dated) *Career Awareness Tours: A work experience strategy step-by-step guide.* Langley, BC: School District #35 (Langley).

Montague, M. and Lund, K. A. (1991) *Job-related Social Skills: A curriculum for adolescents with special needs.* Reston, VA: Exceptional Innovations.

Park, C. C. (1967) *The Siege: The first eight years of an autistic child.* Boston, MA: Little Brown and Company.

Park, C. C. (2001) *Exiting Nirvana: A daughter's life with autism.* Boston, MA: Little Brown and Company.

Saskatchewan Education (1999) *Career Guidance for the Middle Level 6, Self Awareness: A bibliography.* Regina, SK: Saskatchewan Education.

SD #72 Career Development Department (2000) *Resumé Workshop.* Campbell River, BC: Campbell River School District #72.

Smith, N. B. (1969) "Reading for depth." In M. L. King, L. W. Ellinger and W. Wolf (eds) *Critical Reading.* New York: Lippincott.

Websites

www.autismoutreach.ca
The Provincial Outreach Program for Autism and Related Disorders website is designed to help teachers, parents and support staff access information about autism, the BC school system's resources, how the provincial program works, and links to other autism sites. The site also provides a number of web casts that cover pertinent topics related to ASD. This site is supported by the BC Ministry of Education.

www.autism.org
The Center for the Study of Autism (CSA) is located in the Salem/Portland, Oregon area. The Center provides information about autism to parents and professionals, and conducts research on the efficacy of various therapeutic interventions. Much of the Center's research is in collaboration with the Autism Research Institute in San Diego, California.

www.bced.gov.bc.ca/graduation/portfolio
This site is hosted by the Ministry of Education for the Government of British Columbia and provides students, parents and teachers with information about the graduation portfolio, a graduation requirement for students in BC.

http://www.conferenceboard.ca/education/learningtools/employability-skills.htm
The Conference Board of Canada builds leadership capacity by creating and sharing insights on economic trends, public policies and organizational performance. The site offers information on the employability skills required to be successful in the workplace.

www.setbc.org
Special Education Technology is supported by the BC Ministry of Education. It strives to enhance student opportunities, including students with autism, for success by providing access to curriculum through the use of appropriate educational and communication technologies. This site offers a variety of information and supports that help enhance student success at school and in the community.

www.socialsecurity.gov/online/ss-5.html
The US Government Social Security Office site provides information for accessing information and forms to apply for a social security card.

www.hrsdc.gc.ca/en/gateways/topics/sxn-gxr.shtml
This Canadian Government website provides information for accessing information and forms to apply for a social insurance card.